Rescued by
CANBERR

Rescued by the CANBERRA

How the Jones Family's
round-the-world sailing adventure
nearly ended in disaster

Josh and Vicki Jones

DAVID & CHARLES
London Newton Abbot North Pomfret (Vt)

British Library Cataloguing in Publication Data

Jones (*Family*)
Rescued by the Canberra: how the Jones
Family's round-the-world sailing
adventure nearly ended in disaster.
1.Voyages around the world – 1951–
2. Yachts and yachting
I. Title
910.4'1 G419

ISBN 0-7153-9130-5

Typeset by Typesetters (Birmingham) Ltd
Smethwick, West Midlands
and printed in Great Britain
by Billing & Sons Ltd Worcester
for David & Charles Publishers plc
Brunel House Newton Abbot Devon

Published in the United States of America
by David & Charles Inc
North Pomfret Vermont 05053 USA

For Auntie Marne, who helped us through
the magic door.

For all those who helped us along
the paths beyond.

And for all those who helped to pick us up
when we fell.

CONTENTS

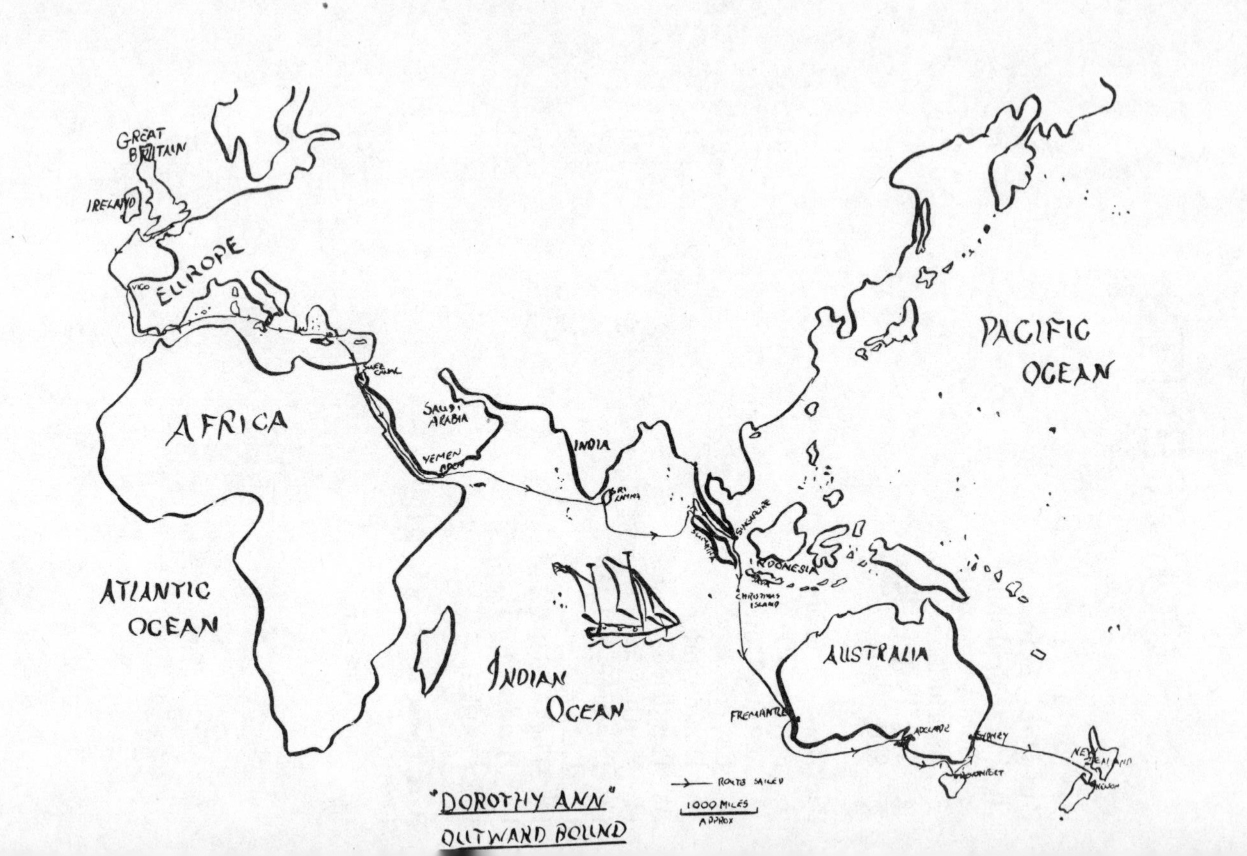

"DOROTHY ANN"
OUTWARD BOUND

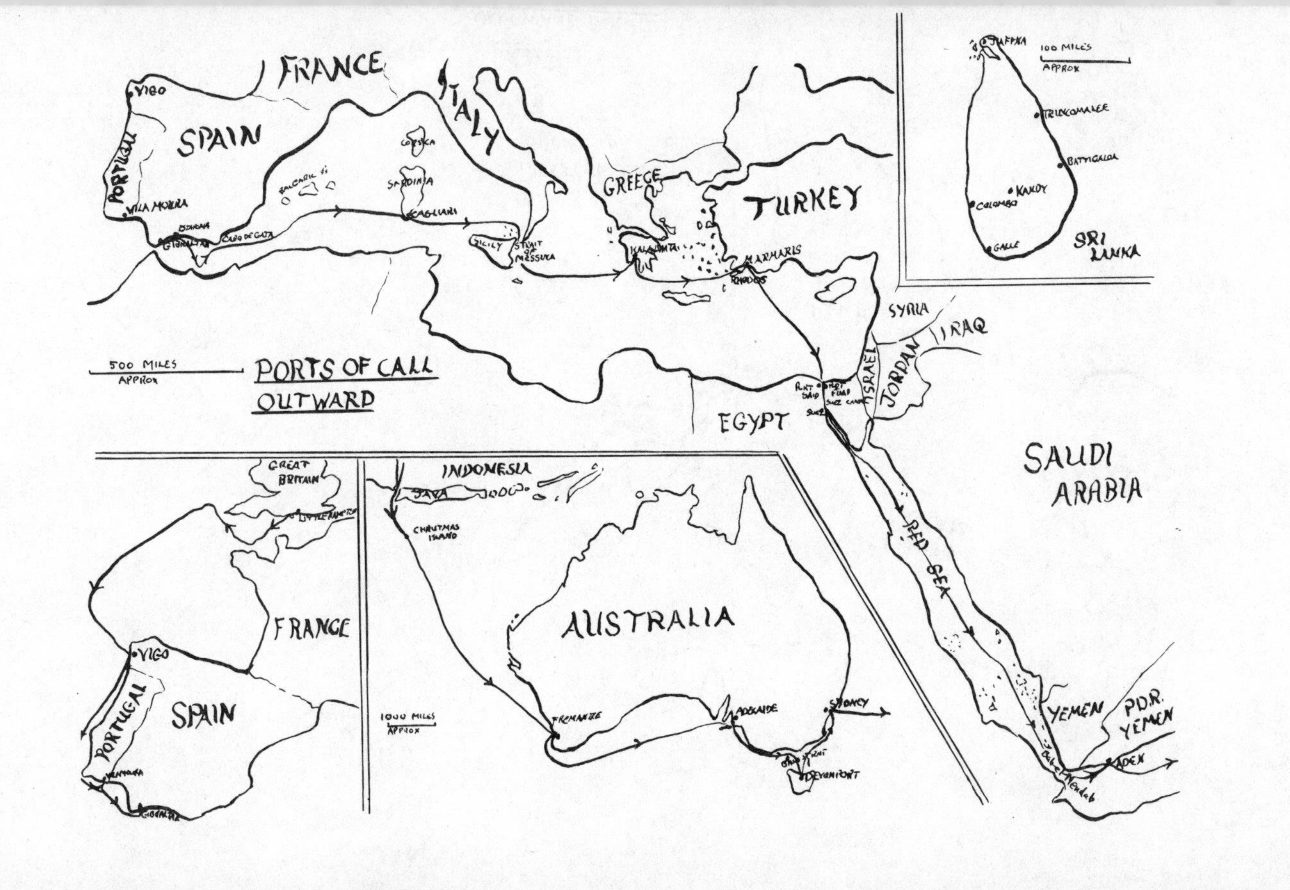
PORTS OF CALL
OUTWARD
500 MILES
APPROX
FRANCE
SPAIN
PORTUGAL
VIGO
VILA MOURA
GIBRALTAR
CABO DE GATA
CORSICA
SARDINIA
CAGLIARI
ITALY
SICILY
STRAIT OF MESSINA
GREECE
TURKEY
MARMARIS
RHODES
SYRIA
IRAQ
ISRAEL
JORDAN
PORT SAID
PORT FUAD
SUEZ CANAL
SUEZ
EGYPT
SAUDI
ARABIA
RED SEA
YEMEN
P.D.R.
YEMEN
ADEN
100 MILES
APPROX
JAFFNA
TRINCOMALEE
BATTICALOA
KANDY
COLOMBO
GALLE
SRI
LANKA
GREAT
BRITAIN
FRANCE
VIGO
SPAIN
PORTUGAL
GIBRALTAR
INDONESIA
JAVA
CHRISTMAS
ISLAND
AUSTRALIA
ADELAIDE
SYDNEY
DEVONPORT
1000 MILES
APPROX

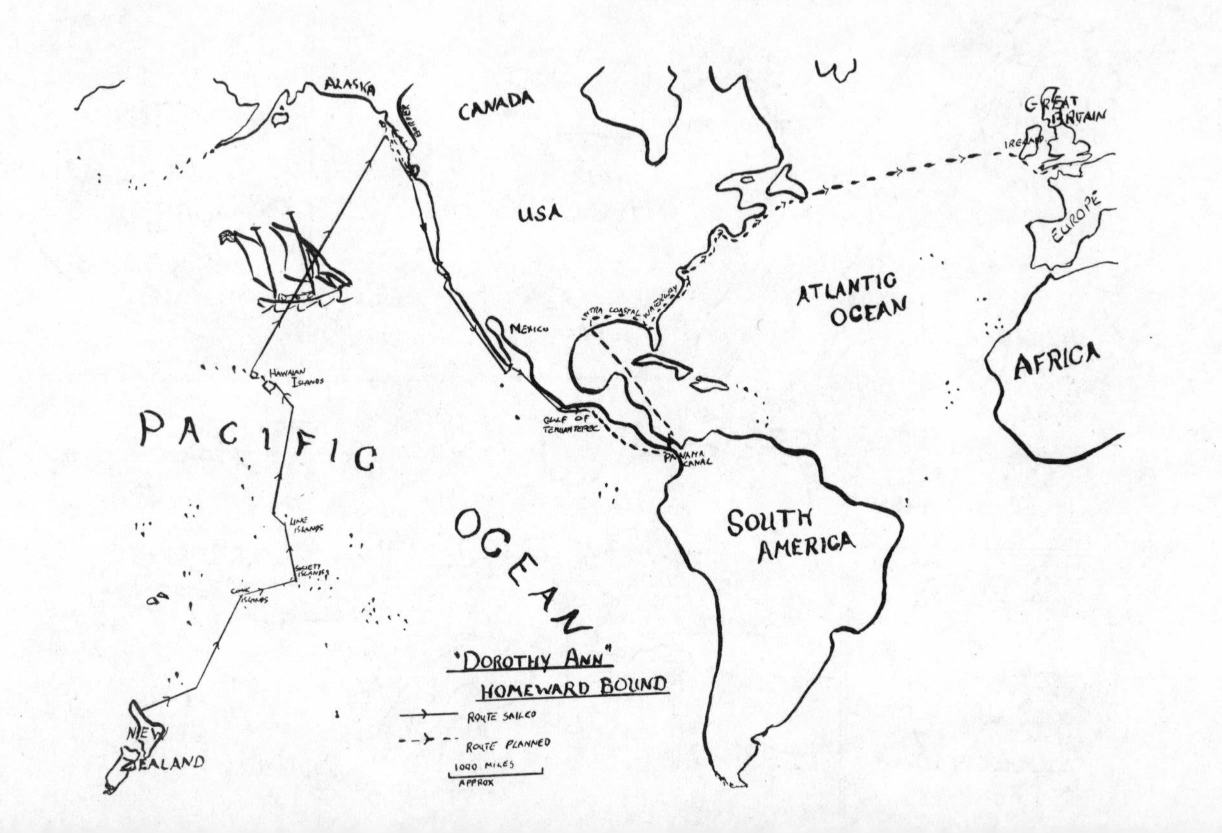
"DOROTHY ANN"
HOMEWARD BOUND
ROUTE SAILED
ROUTE PLANNED
1000 MILES
APPROX
ALASKA
CANADA
USA
MEXICO
GULF OF TEHUANTEPEC
INTRA COASTAL WATERWAY
PANAMA CANAL
PACIFIC OCEAN
ATLANTIC OCEAN
SOUTH AMERICA
AFRICA
EUROPE
GREAT BRITAIN
IRELAND
HAWAIIAN ISLANDS
LINE ISLANDS
SOCIETY ISLANDS
COOK ISLANDS
NEW ZEALAND

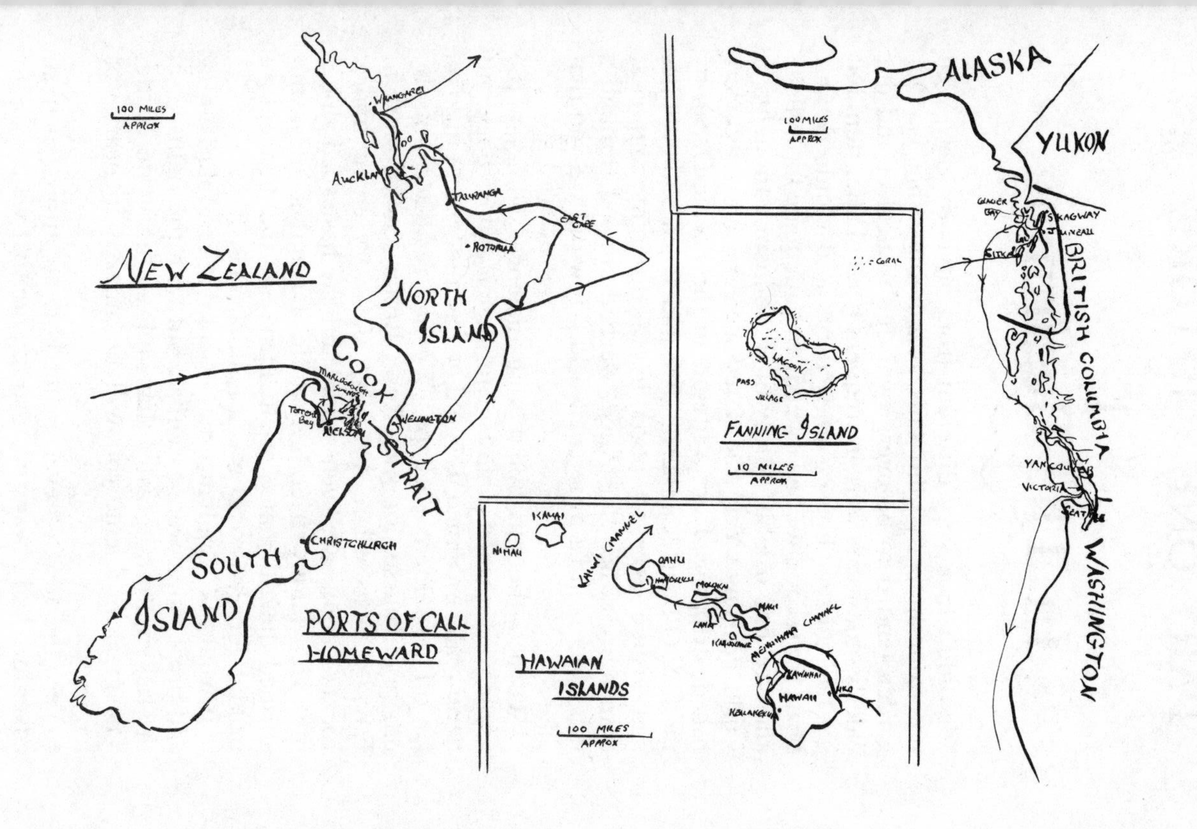

PORTS OF CALL
HOMEWARD
NEW ZEALAND
100 MILES
APPROX
NORTH ISLAND
SOUTH ISLAND
COOK STRAIT
WHANGAREI
AUCKLAND
TAURANGA
ROTORUA
EAST CAPE
WELLINGTON
NELSON
MARLBOROUGH SOUNDS
CHRISTCHURCH
FANNING ISLAND
10 MILES
APPROX
LAGOON
PASS
VILLAGE
CORAL
HAWAIIAN ISLANDS
100 MILES
APPROX
KAUAI
NIIHAU
KAIWI CHANNEL
OAHU
HONOLULU
MOLOKAI
MAUI
LANAI
KAHOOLAWE
HAWAII
HILO
KEALAKEKUA
ALASKA
YUKON
BRITISH COLUMBIA
WASHINGTON
100 MILES
APPROX
GLACIER BAY
SKAGWAY
JUNEAU
SITKA
VANCOUVER
VICTORIA

PART ONE BEFORE . . .

1
In The Beginning

We didn't look very different from anybody else. Well not from anybody who sails as a hobby, that is. Our garden tended to be overgrown due to neglect and our elderly motor cars were in frequent need of attention, but we had jobs, a house, dogs, debts and children. Our boat, the second we had owned, was adequate for holiday and weekend use but hardly likely to inspire thoughts of world cruising. Yet when, seven years later, we were fished, dripping, from a liferaft in the Pacific Ocean by the P & O liner "Canberra", we had sailed 35,000 miles and visited over 50 ports in 18 different countries. Somehow, rather like Alice, we had slipped through a magic door into a different world. How did we find that door?

We had thought about long distance sailing in the vague way in which many an "armchair sailor" does, but never really imagined it would be feasible, except in some far off retirement perhaps. We had read accounts by others of course; Sir Alec Rose, Robin Knox-Johnston, David Lewis, Clare Francis, and very many more. Vicki's parents are keen sailors and she has sailed all her life. Her family friends include a number of distinguished long-distance yachtsmen, so the concept of making long passages was a familiar one.

It would be tough at times of course; careful planning and preparation were essential, but with the right vessel the risks were no greater that in any other walk of life. The great problem, you will be amazed to hear, was money.

Yes, the idea of ever being able to afford such an adventure had always been so remote that we had never seriously thought of it. Instead, we had slowly acquired the elements of a normal family life, though we took our weekend and holiday sailing seriously, studying navigation and seamanship, sailing in all weathers (though not, I hasten to add, in winter) reading and thinking more, perhaps, than we realised. Our children, having sailed from infancy, regarded boats and sailing as a normal and familiar part of life.

Yet it was money or, oddly enough, the lack of it, which finally opened the magic door.

Vicki's parents had emigrated to Australia in 1969. They had visited us in England twice since then and we had promised to make a return visit within the next three years. Like a lot of promises for the future, this one had seemed easy enough at the time, but now we were faced with the fact that it ought not to be put off much longer. We were standing in the kitchen of our home at Wokingham in Berkshire, a long way from the sea, when the fateful decision was made.

It was that rather flat period just after Christmas when the presents have all been opened, the guests have departed and the sight of yet another turkey sandwich produces a great lack of enthusiasm. We had decided that it was time to come to grips with this problem of going to Sydney for the promised visit and were going over the cost yet again. For the five of us the air fares alone would wipe out our savings and we would have to borrow as much again. Then how about the time? If we could both take our annual holidays together, if both our employers would let us take all our leave entitlement for two years at the same time, we could spend about six weeks in Australia at most. Then no more holidays for two years and very little spare cash too. Neither of us was very happy about the idea, but we had said we would go and that was that. Was there any alternative? We had been feeling rather fidgety for some time. Our two dogs had died, so we had been talking of sailing abroad now that there were no problems of quarantine restrictions or expensive kennelling to consider. I, however, had always argued that the cost of visiting Northern Europe, which was as far as we could hope to go in a normal summer holiday, was not worth the prospects. The weather and scenery are no better than in England and the costs and difficulties if we had any mishap might be horrendous. It seemed to me rather like risking five pounds on a horse in order to maybe win a shilling. Now, the conversation went:

"This trip to Australia will wipe out our savings."

"Well what are we saving for?"

"To buy a bigger boat."

"What for?"

"So that we can sail longer distances."

Pause.

"Australia is a longer distance." Rather longer pause, with marked lack of breathing.

This offered a much more glittering prize. For a much greater outlay of course, but we might find some way to afford it. Over the years we had paid off quite a lot of our mortgage and we might sell the house, put aside a sum for our eventual return, and put the rest toward paying for the journey. There might be other ways to raise money. Was sponsorship possible? Could we write about our experiences during or even before the voyage? Could we do it? Would we?

A lot of dreams pass through our minds in this way; we smile at our foolishness in imagining such things, shrug our shoulders and get on with everyday life, doubting later if it ever could have been. This one I grabbed firmly by the scruff of its neck as it almost slipped past. We would do this thing now or resign ourselves to a life in which our most important decision would be which television programme to watch. We needed a formal commitment. I held out my hand to Vicki and said "Shall we do it; sail to Australia?"

I don't think the pause was very long, though it seemed so at the time. However, we both knew that the commitment, once made, would be binding on both of us. It was no light decision. She smiled, took my hand and said one word. "Yes."

We started to plan at once. We decided that we would need a third adult so that we could always respond to the needs of the boat and the children simultaneously if need be. Robert (Bob) Smith is an old friend who had helped us to launch our first boat. He had sailed with us and owned his own boat. Most importantly, the children had known him all their lives and trusted him completely. A bachelor, with very few commitments, he agreed at once to join us. Together we set target dates; six months to find a suitable boat, leave England the following April. It didn't quite work out that way, but we started out well.

Vicki went boat hunting. I can't stand the Earls Court boat show myself but both she and Bob trudged through the crowds and enquired about vessels which we were unlikely ever to afford. At that time we were considering trying to find sponsors, but we soon realised that running around trying to get someone to pay for our pleasures was an activity which appealed to none of us. We had always paid our own way and we would somehow do so this time. The search was now directed to the second-hand boat market.

We created a planning system, opening files for Finance, Voyage planning, Preparation, and Concurrent activities, such as the sale of our existing boats and houses. We prepared budgets which never balanced and later became too busy to keep the files in order, but it seemed very systematic at the start and gave a business-like feeling to the whole project.

It did enable us to see what needed to be done and in what order. It also made it possible to divide the work up between us, a necessity because Bob lived at Tiptree in Essex and could not run to and fro frequently between our house and his. Bob undertook the task of gathering information about possible routes, searching through not only books and magazines but also the mass of unpublished reports held in the library of the Cruising Association, at St Katherine's Dock in London. He produced three wonderfully detailed summaries of Physical and Political obstacles, Weather, Passage Lengths and Estimated Times, and Places of Interest en route.

Once the route was agreed he obtained and updated all

our Navigational Charts, Pilot books, Lists of Lights and Radio Signals, Sight Reduction Tables, for Sextant Navigation and so forth. Vicki investigated Visa and Medical requirements along the route, making all the necessary applications and appointments, and somehow getting all of us to the right offices at the right times.

We decided to sell both Bob's and our house and buy a small cottage with the money we intended to keep for our return. This would be crammed with our joint possessions and would hopefully appreciate in value as property prices continued their inexorable rise. This triggered off another mass of detail problems. How would we invest the capital for the project so as to earn interest and stretch it as far as possible, yet be able to get money when and where we needed it? Visits to the Bank, Solicitors, drawing up Wills, arranging Powers of Attorney. . . . we almost forgot what Sailing was.

Of course we all had full time jobs and, despite some help from me, Vicki had the house and the children to cope with. She was also Membership Secretary of the Eventide Owners Association, a club for people owning boats of similar design to our own, and this created quite a workload. Despite this, she and Bob found time to attend evening classes in Celestial Navigation.

All these activities continued for some time after we found the right boat for the voyage and began the long job of fitting out and preparation. Planning continued to the end, though it was rather sporadic at times. Bob made careful appraisals of equipment and costs for Underwater Swimming, Fishing and Photography. Vicki tracked down Boat and Medical insurers, by no means an easy task.

And what did I do? Apart from helping Vicki to cope at home, I tried to plan and co-ordinate our joint efforts and at the same time to keep our aged and worn cars and domestic appliances working. Also, once we had the boat the more physically taxing parts of the refitting became my share, though Vicki did a great deal and Bob helped whenever he could. Writing about it now it doesn't seem very much. At the time it became totally exhausting.

2
Horses for Courses

Choosing a boat is rather like choosing a spouse. You may have some well formed views as to what would be ideal, but no one but you is likely to see much connection between your stated preferences and your actual choice. In both cases there is the question of availability too. The other party generally has some say in the matter as well and boats, though inanimate, can exert a powerful influence on the sailor. We have found on the whole that the true, hard bitten, professional sailor is a far greater romantic than those "yachtsmen" who buy plastic boats by the yard and drive them round race courses at weekends, like motor cars; but there are some remarkable exceptions even in the latter group.

Our previous boats had been sailed on the East coast of England, operating from our base at the Maldon Little Ship Club, on the Blackwater river in Essex. That is an area of shallow waters and many shoals, with few places having enough water to float a boat at low tide.

Shallow boats with double keels, which sit upright when aground, are a good choice for such waters. There is a loss of sailing performance, but that is not too great a handicap for local cruising over short distances. Stowage space is limited too, but adequate for a short holiday voyage. Of course one could buy or build a bigger boat, but costs tend to relate to length rather than volume, whether it be the initial price or subsequent mooring and maintenance costs.

So a smaller, deeper boat is often preferred by deep water sailors. Our existing boat "Geisha", a twin keeled, shallow draught, 24 foot long "Eventide" design had served us well, but she was quite unsuitable for what we now intended to do.

We considered multi-hulled boats, catamarans and trimarans. They are fast and spacious and many Ocean passages have been safely accomplished in them. One major drawback is that if they should be heeled over in extreme conditions, beyond a critical point, they will overturn and be impossible to right. It is important therefore to choose a well proven design specifically intended for Ocean Cruising. It must also be large enough to carry full cruising equipment without being overloaded. Most long distance cruising boats become well laden with stores, water, souvenirs, diving gear, and so on. If a multihull is overloaded it will lose the ability to sail fast, which is its principal attraction. A large well designed and built multihull is costly to buy.

A new boat of conventional, monohull, design, about 40 feet long, would have suited us very well. It would also have cost us about £60,000 for the basic boat, plus several thousands more for equipment. Since our total available cash at that time was just over £3,000 we needed to find an alternative solution. We wrote to yacht brokers and yards, bought yachting magazines crammed with advertisements and prepared to spend many weekends plodding around chilly and unsalubrious neighbourhoods looking at overpriced and unseaworthy vessels.

Among the growing pile of yacht brokers' leaflets which was taking over our living space, along with magazines, boat show catalogues, maps, charts, geography and history books, accounts of voyages, and much else, there one day appeared a description, with photograph attatched, of an old wooden ketch. This boat, we learned from broker "Stormy" Davies' description, was an absolute paragon among vessels. Lovingly cared for by a single owner until his death, still owned by his family, she had, it seemed, not a single defect and was ideal for world cruising.

Regrettably, I cannot precisely reproduce "Stormy"'s exact prose as it now lies, complete with that appealing photograph, half a mile under the Pacific Ocean.

We had some experience of interpreting yacht brokers' claims over the years since we had first contemplated boat ownership; in fact we had a useful translation technique which we had developed for interpreting house agentese into English, and we found the languages very similar.

In this case we concluded that the vessel concerned was not actually resting on the bottom, but that it might well go there soon. However, she was 35 feet long, flush decked, and, most important, we could probably raise most of the asking price. We made an appointment and drove to Barry in South Wales on a grey, drizzling day in January 1980 to meet "Stormy" Davies and see "Dorothy Ann" for the first time.

I wonder if the dreadful sadness which I feel as I write this is for the loss of our beloved ship, or is it just because of the memory of the years which seem to have passed so rapidly since? She was to give us an experience so wonderful that nothing in our future lives can ever surpass it. Even on that dull, wet day in Wales, we felt her magic.

Magic. That word keeps jumping into my mind without conscious thought. The magic was not achieved without a lot of hard work, but the promise of it was always there to spur us on. We drove down to the docks, following "Stormy"'s car down the steep hill on which the town of Barry is built. Down roads paved with oblong stone "setts", past the huge, impressive Merchant Naval College, a symbol of the town's past importance and seafaring traditions, to the old graving dock; now the home of a varied array of small vessels.

"Dorothy Ann" nestled snugly against the dock wall, patiently awaiting our coming. The dock basin is prevented from emptying when the tide falls by a lock. However the level in the basin does fall gradually as ships pass out through the lock and at the time of our arrival the water level was fairly low. Thus we were presented with an aerial view of "Dorothy Ann" as we looked down on her from the quayside.

As I have said, she was flush decked; that is, her sides were built up to the full height which a "cabin top" would rise to and the deck was therefore unbroken across the full width of the boat, except for a skylight in the centre. This gave an immediate impression of size and power, which was no illusion. "Stormy" unlocked the main hatch and removed the washboards which formed the main entrance. The scene below was less inspiring.

Beads of water clung to every surface. The floorboards had been raised to aid ventilation, revealing a jumble of rusty iron ballast blocks. I pushed open the sliding door to the galley cupboard and it fell out onto the floor. A narrow passageway leading forward past a massive table, its surface green and cracked, was partially blocked by a long, heavy bowsprit and an assortment of lighter wooden spars.

Drawers were mouldy and jammed. Paint peeled from the deckhead above. "Stormy" removed wooden panels, revealing a virtually new diesel engine, its paint and bright plating gleaming in the gloom. It started at the touch of a key and thudded happily away. Sensibly, he then left us to make our examination in peace. Love affairs, even with ships, need privacy to develop properly. We set to work to make our initial survey.

All I required to know at this stage was whether the boat was worth the asking price, that is, if it proved unsuitable for our purposes, could we at least expect to resell it, preferably at a profit. We would need to know a lot more than any ordinary survey would reveal before setting off into the unknown.

Every part of the hull which was not blocked off by furniture or panelling was probed and tested for weakness or rot. We found some decay in the framing of the hull, where rainwater had seeped through the deck seams and into the oak. There were a few deck planks which would need renewal, and a major beam across the rear of the cabin needed replacing. There were bound to be some other weaknesses, but the main structure was as sound as a bell, despite the depressing appearance. We locked up, returned the keys and went home to consider.

There was quite a lot to think about. We had begun by thinking in terms of a new catamaran; a fast, light vessel, requiring little preparation and able to complete the voyage in a relatively short time. Now we were considering the opposite end of the scale; a slow, heavy vessel which would need a lot of time to prepare.

I had thought perhaps of asking for unpaid leave of absence from my work, but I felt that even if that were possible, two years would be the maximum I could hope to get. With this boat we would need three years at least for the voyage and probably more. Could we handle the old fashioned, heavy rig? Luckily I had begun my sailing with gaff rigged boats on the Norfolk Broads, so, unlike Vicki and Bob, who had both sailed only the modern Bermudan rig, I was familiar with the essentials of sailing that type. Also the ketch rig, having the sail area divided fairly evenly over two masts, has reasonably light sails and spars.

"Dorothy Ann" had a deep, full length keel combined with a well rounded hull shape and an almost vertical bow and stern. This meant a lot more space inside than in more modern hull shapes, especially with the built up topsides and flush deck, which gave full height right across the interior. It also meant poor manoeuvrability, particularly when motoring, and the ability to roll stupendously at the slightest provocation.

These latter points were only apparent later. We went through the motions of solemnly discussing pros and cons, but there could only be one outcome. We were hooked. We spent a week resisting temptation, but on the first day of February 1980 Vicki and I became Joint Owners of the 64 shares of "Dorothy Ann", the number into which ownership of ships is traditionally divided.

We now had two boats, two cars, a house, a mortgage, and a large bank loan. "Geisha" was advertised for sale, though we would need to complete our winter refit in order to get the best possible price. The weather was not going to be suitable for doing a great deal of work out of doors until March, at least, so for the time being we collected "Dorothy Ann"s mattresses and cushions from the home of Mrs Chubb, widow of the original owner, after whom the boat was named, and took them home to store and refurbish.

We continued to pursue our other activities of course, since, as I have said, we don't like just one thing to blot out everything else. The Eventide Owners Association held occasional meetings at the Cruising Association's premises in London and at one of these meetings Ross gave a talk to the members.

Ross is an Australian who had built a Waterwitch, another design represented by the association, in Australia and sailed it to England with his wife and family. They had travelled by a similar route to that which we intended to take, in the opposite direction; we wanted very much to learn anything which they could tell us about ocean sailing and wasted no time in inviting them to come and visit us. This they did, on several occasions. Their advice was invaluable, their humour and commonsense even more so. They were doing as a family what we were intending to do as a family, and doing it very successfully.

3
Interlude

"Dorothy Ann" was at Barry, in South Wales. "Geisha" was at Maldon, in Essex. They were just about as far apart as they could be and we were living about half way in between. In distance we were nearer to Maldon, but we had to drive across London to get there, which made for a slow journey. Most of the journey to Barry could be done on the M4 motorway, a fast but boring trip. Both routes were hard on cars laden with people, boat's gear, tools, paint and food.

We couldn't do much about "Geisha", but with any luck she would soon be sold anyway. She was safe enough, having been hauled out as usual to spend the winter high and dry in Tom Hedgecock's boatyard. Being a plywood hull there was not the problem of planks drying out and shrinking which makes keeping a planked boat out of the water a tricky operation.

Obviously the thing to do was to bring "Dorothy Ann" nearer to home. We wondered if it would be possible to bring her up the Thames, to Reading, and if so where it would be possible to lift her out under cover, at reasonable cost, so that we could work on the hull if need be. But most of the refitting would need to be done afloat, so that the hull planking did not dry out and become leaky. The Thames at Reading is fresh water, would that cause damage to the planking? Was there enough of the canal system intact to allow passage from the Bristol Channel or the Avon to the Thames, or would we have to sail right up the English Channel and North Sea to the Thames Estuary and then motor all the way back, through numerous locks? In any case there would be bridges to pass under, so the masts would have to be removed and stored elsewhere or transported expensively overland.

The canal idea proved to be impractical and the long voyage to the Thames Estuary was too far for us to attempt at this stage. We decided to find a mooring on the South coast, if possible, and to do sufficient work at Barry to assure ourselves that the journey there could be safely accomplished. I expected difficulty in finding a mooring at all, in that crowded and popular area and I was right. Once again though, our path was magically cleared for us. A drying mooring in Chichester harbour had just become vacant, and the harbour master was inclined to favour the restoration and preservation of old boats, so it became ours.

Meanwhile, we drove to Barry on one weekend and worked on "Dorothy Ann", drove to Maldon the next and worked on "Geisha" and spent the following weekend usually maintaining our worn-out cars. Then back to Barry and so on.

There were exceptions of course. One weekend we collected Ross and Margaret and set off for the Beaulieu Boat Jumble Sale, an open air market for an incredible variety of boat equipment, old and new, which is held annually at Lord Montague's estate in Hampshire. We had a hectic and enjoyable day during which we bought a dinghy complete with outboard motor and road trailer. It was as well that we did because our combined load of anchors, sails, rolls of vinyl, ropes, blocks, sextants, and other desirable things could not possibly have fitted into the car. We piled them into the dinghy, lashed them down and headed back up the A3.

The final memorable event of the day occurred as I drove Ross and Margaret back to St Katharine's Dock. A brake pad failed on the car, at about Piccadilly Circus I think, and I had to drive very gingerly indeed all the way to Tower Bridge, then all the way back and home to Wokingham. The following weekend was a car maintenance weekend again.

After we had mopped up most of the condensation in "Dorothy Ann" and the weather grew warmer so that no great further quantity was produced, the interior began to look quite inviting. The deck seams however were not totally rain proof and we could not see much point in doing any work on the interior until they were recaulked and made water tight. The way that these seams are caulked is to hammer a tightly twisted cotton yarn into a "V" shaped gap between the planks, so that it will swell when wet and crush into the wood at either side, forming a tight seal. The cotton is then covered with putty, tar, or some form of patent sealer.

The putty in "Dorothy Ann"s deck seams was old and cracked in places and had been patched up here and there with synthetic resin compounds. It was likely that the cotton was old and had lost its strength. Before we could do anything about that, the putty had to come out. Vicki began to tackle that job, trying to remove the old putty with a hand tool. It was a tremendous struggle and in some places the putty stuck tightly to the plank edges, tending to damage the wood as it came out. It was obvious that we needed a better method if we were to get anywhere. We tried using a circular saw attachment on an electric drill, but after blunting three saw blades in a few inches of putty we stopped and thought again. Finally we bought a masonry cutting wheel and, to our great relief, that did the job. It was still quite slow though, as Vicki had to be careful not to damage the planking and there was a lot of cleaning off by hand still needed. We worked on a small area at a time, Vicki cleaning out the seam, myself driving in the new cotton and puttying over it, so that when we had to leave, or if rain threatened, the seam was protected.

That job and many others were finally done and we ventured out into the dock basin to try a few manoeuvres. The wind was light and there was not a great deal of room to travel for long in any one direction, but it all went quite smoothly. The next thing was to clean off and examine the underwater hull. To do this we locked out into the Bristol Channel and sailed a short distance to Barry old harbour, an empty expanse of hard sand on which, as the tide receded, "Dorothy Ann" stood upright, supported by a pair of strong wooden "legs" bolted to her sides. As the water fell we scrubbed off the coating of weed and assorted sea life which a boat always attracts. There was not very much, really. It was obvious that she had still been cared for, although little used in the three years since the elder Mr Chubb had died.

The planking slowly dried in the weak May sunshine and we examined it carefully. The paint was in good condition, though because bottom paint is intended to dissolve slowly, releasing chemicals to inhibit weed and barnacle growth, a fresh coat would be needed for the coming season. There was one trickle of water from a point on one of the seams, indicating that the caulking needed attention, but it was very small and for the time being I simply drove in the existing caulking a little more tightly and added more putty to fill the depression which that caused. We peered and tapped at the planking, but could detect no sign of decay or weakness. Soon we had applied a fresh coat of anti-fouling paint, the tide flowed in and we returned to Barry dock for the last time.

The following weekend we arrived at the dock, laden with provisions for a week's voyage. That really meant enough to feed the six of us for three weeks if need be, because Vicki always makes sure that we have an ample reserve. The most dangerous place for a boat in bad weather is near land, so we have always liked to make sure that we can remain safely out at sea if conditions make it dangerous to try and reach port. With plenty of food, water and fuel, there is no temptation to act foolishly and rush for port.

We lashed the dinghy on deck, filled our water tanks to the brim and motored out through the lock. We wanted to get as much information as possible about ourselves and our boat during this journey. We would make the passage direct to Chichester without putting in to any intermediate ports. Sailing day and night, we would test our watchkeeping system and our night sailing ability. Our consumption of stores and water would be carefully monitored. We should get a reasonable idea of "Dorothy Ann"s performance under a variety of wind and sea conditions. By sailing a direct course, with no attempt to follow the coastline, we would be out of sight of land quite a lot of the time; this would give us a chance to practise our Astro navigation. It was an important test.

Before setting out we wanted to check our compass for accuracy. We had studied the chart and identified some conspicuous features ashore which would give us our true bearings. We began to motor the boat on various courses, checking the compass readings against these known bearings and preparing the "deviation table" from which future corrections for error would be made. For a while all went well, but unnoticed by us as we concentrated on our measurements, a rising wind was beginning to build up the seas. Suddenly, as we turned on a course parallel to the waves, we began to roll vigorously. Everyone began to feel queasy and I realised that we ought to get sail on the boat to steady the motion; also, it was getting late. We ought to be getting on our way in order to get well clear of the land by nightfall. The compass, mounted well clear of all metal, was error free anyway. Turning into wind, "Dorothy Ann" headed out of the bay and into the Bristol Channel.

Even motoring gently into the seas the motion was quite violent. Bob had a struggle to hoist the mainsail and I had to go forward and give him a hand with the last few feet of halliard. He then took over the tiller whilst I tried to untie the lashings on the mizen sail. I seemed to spend most of the time clinging to the boom and gaff as they swung wildly from side to side due to the rolling, despite the steadying effect of the mainsail. Wrenched off my feet and swung out over the water from one side to the other, I was very glad that my life line was securely clipped on. After what seemed like several hours the cords came untied at last and the sail was hoisted. Bobby went below and I was left alone at the helm as we headed into the coming night. We ought to have set the foresails too, but for the time being I was content to jog along quietly until conditions improved and we recovered our strength.

It was only an evening breeze. Later it died down and by dawn we were forging slowly across the Bristol

Channel with all sail set, toward the North Devon coast where "Dorothy Ann" had been built over 40 years ago. We settled quickly into our seagoing routine, working our watches, taking our turns at the helm, preparing meals, taking sights. After our rather uncomfortable start we had light winds and calms, slowly making our way down past Land's End and turning eastward along the English Channel. It remained pleasant until we reached the vicinity of Portland Bill, when a rising wind, which at first gave us a good enjoyable burst of speed, gradually moved round to blow from dead ahead. Forced to tack outward from the land, we gradually reduced sail as the wind rose further. Quite suddenly we were among the Channel shipping. Big ships, even where there is no regulation, tend to all take much the same path. In the narrow waters of the English Channel there are areas where the traffic is regulated by law, as if on roads. We were not in such an area, but none the less common sense dictated that we should keep clear of larger vessels if possible. A small yacht in high seas is remarkably hard to see and although we had a radar reflector we could not assume that the echo which it produced would be visible against the "clutter" which rough water produces on a radar screen.

We had quite a lot to learn about "Dorothy Ann" and some of it took a long time. The combination of sails which we were using was not properly balanced, so that she refused to turn onto the opposite tack and head inshore away from the traffic. We finally used the motor to help her round. It was easy enough to do that, but it seemed very unseamanlike to rely on the auxiliary motor in a vessel intended to be powered principally by sail. The Chubb family had sailed her successfully for years with no power other than her sails; it was up to us to learn to do the same. Up to a point we did so, though after 35,000 miles we were still learning more every day. For the moment, I reduced sail further by taking in the jib. That stopped the bows from tending to dig into the waves and produced a pleasanter motion. My watch having ended, I went below for a few hours' sleep.

When I next came on deck the sun was shining and the seas were moderate. Vicki and Bob had navigated us accurately to the Isle of Wight and we slipped easily down the Solent to anchor behind Hurst Fort for the night. This was necessary because Chichester harbour has a sand bar across the entrance and we would need to wait for the tide to rise sufficiently next day for us to cross over it. In the morning we made a leisurely start and timed our arrival at the bar so that we could enter the harbour safely and without haste. The voyage, with its calms and head winds, had taken six days. The total distance would have been about 350 miles had we not been obliged to tack. In fact it was a very accurate demonstration of "Dorothy Ann"s average speed in variable conditions, though she could travel a good deal faster given the right combination of wind and sea. We used the rest of that weekend to settle "Dorothy Ann" in her new home.

A few weeks later we sailed her on to the "Hard" at Ichenor (a hard surfaced area of the shore, used also as a launching area for boats carried on trailers) where she stood once again supported by her "legs" whilst a professional surveyor gave her a thorough examination. He produced a modest list of recommendations, none of which were of any surprise to us, and we returned her once again to her berth. Up to this point things had gone fairly well to plan. We were about to stumble upon the first real obstacle.

We needed to find a friendly boatyard where we could have "Dorothy Ann" lifted out of the water and stored under cover for protection from the weather, whilst we did some work which could not be done when afloat. We were happy to pay for the lifting and storage, but we wanted to do the work ourselves. Apart from the simple desire to KNOW, from first hand experience, that something on which our lives depended had been done properly, we could not afford to pay inflated prices for the work. This was a problem. Some yards would not let owners do any work at all. Others were only open during the working week when, amazing though they found it, we were at work.

In the meantime however there was plenty we could get on with. The entire hull above the waterline was stripped to the bare wood, every plank fastening exposed, examined, treated against corrosion and resealed, and the hull repainted with several coats of primer, undercoat and white gloss paint. New rudder fittings, patterned on the old, worn ones, were made up by a blacksmith from wrought iron, which the ever resourceful Vicki obtained from a demolition site, on her way to her work in Reading. Ross and Margaret came down with us and helped to dismantle some of the interior fittings which we needed to change. The children disappeared for long hours about their mysterious affairs on the neighbouring marsh. It was a fairly small area, with no natural hazards, but sufficient bramble bushes and tall grass to provide a miniature jungle through which they could travel by paths impassable to mere adults. They stained their faces purple consuming endless quantities of blackberries, occasionally bringing some for us. Rabbits abounded there and would ignore the casual passer by who did not make excessive noise. In many ways it was an idyllic summer. The weather was obligingly dry, allowing me to replace the defective area of deck planking, as well as getting the hull repainting done without mishap. Autumn came and passed almost unnoticed as the fine weather held. Then, as the first cold breaths of winter began to be felt, Vicki found our boatyard.

Andy and John had founded their business, "Bevis Boat Services" in a huge, chilly shed on the bank of the Arun river, at Littlehampton in Sussex. Vicki had spotted an article about this new enterprise in a yachting magazine and decided to investigate. We knew the town fairly well; I was born and grew up in Sussex and my parents were living in Littlehampton when Vicki and I first met. It was quite near to Chichester, so moving the boat would be no problem (or so we innocently thought). It seemed another good omen, and so it was.

Vicki returned from Littlehampton with encouraging

news. John and Andy, she said, knew a thing or three about boats, in fact they knew far more about them than we were ever likely to. They had both owned and sailed vessels of traditional construction, similar to but larger than ours, and they were interested in what we were trying to do. Their main business was servicing the local fishing fleet, but they would be delighted to have us there. We could do all our own work, or use their services if we wished. They were open for business from seven A.M. to seven P.M. and often later, seven days a week. The charges which they proposed were reasonable and within our budget. We would be welcome as soon as we wished. And the catch in this unbelievable good fortune? There wasn't one.

Just before Christmas 1980 we decided to take a break one weekend, going over to Canvey island in Essex to see how Ross and Margaret were getting on. They were at the yard in Benfleet where we had bought "Geisha", doing some repairs to their Waterwitch "Girl Morgan". It was snowing when we arrived, with a bitterly cold east wind blowing. Ross looked almost blue with cold as he worked alongside the boat with no protection from the elements. Margaret had been suffering from bronchitis and looked far from well. We persuaded them to spend the Christmas holidays with us at Wokingham, where we could offer comfort and central heating. We would have been quite hurt if they had not come, something which we tried to remember when we were embarrassed by the generosity shown to us on our later travels. However, they agreed to come and their son Jim was also able to travel down from Yorkshire, where he was taking an apprenticeship. We had a wonderfully enjoyable Christmas together, later driving them to Heathrow to fly home, earn some more cash in warmer surroundings, and return later, in the summertime.

4
The Testing Time

We decided that Bob and I would sail "Dorothy Ann" round to Chichester, leaving Vicki and the children at Wokingham. They didn't think much of this and didn't hesitate to say so. In principle I agreed with them. By and large we do things together or we don't do them at all. But as I pointed out, in this case, since we had partly stripped the interior of the boat, it was going to be fairly uncomfortable. Also, it was winter and Vicki has no love of cold weather. She will wear an overcoat in July if the sun goes in. Mention of possible frost silenced all further argument and we got ready to go. It was not so easy though. Gales blew for the next two weekends and we had to wait for an improvement in the weather.

It was the first weekend in January 1981, when we finally set out. With the harbour master's permission we had moved "Dorothy Ann" to a large buoy, so that we could get underway at any state of the tide. On our own mooring we had floated only for an hour or so at the top of the spring tides. At neap tides we could not get out at all, but remained in a little pool which "Dorothy Ann" had created for herself in the mud. Our plan was to sail down to the harbour mouth, then anchor and wait until the water was deep enough to cross the bar. We would then have about 12 hours in which to reach Littlehampton, crossing the bar there and entering the river Arun with the next rising tide. The weather forecast was for moderate winds from the south-west. We could look forward to a pleasant, easy sail.

It started quite well. We drove down to Ichenor on a peaceful Friday evening and rowed out to "Dorothy Ann". We checked the bilges for water, needing only a few pump strokes to clear them; then motored down to the harbour mouth as planned, anchored safely to one side of the channel and went below for supper. Later I came up to check that all was well before going to sleep. The evening was still, cold and silent; there was a thin film of ice on the deck. I checked the anchor chain and looked around. Nothing moved. Some cottage lights glowed invitingly in the distance. There would be no traffic in the channel until there was sufficient depth of water over the bar for us to leave. I checked the riding light just the same. It was filled with oil and burned clearly. Going down to the warmth of the saloon I turned in. Bob was already in his bunk.

When I next came on deck, at about three a.m. a light breeze was blowing. The ice had gone and the air felt milder. We got under way, motoring slowly from one dimly lit buoy to the next. It is fairly easy to overlook one buoy in a winding channel and unintentionally cut a corner; easier still if one of them happens to be unlit for any reason. So we went cautiously. We had plenty of time and there was no point in going aground. By the time it was light we were clear of the entrance, with all sail set; heading for the Nab tower. The wind was freshening and it looked like being a good day.

It didn't look good for much longer. The wind continued to increase so that by the time we cleared the Nab we were reefing our sails. Bob was feeling his usual seasickness and the wind began to go round from south-west to south, then south-east and further eastward so that I could no longer steer a course clear of the jagged reefs which extend to seaward between Chichester harbour and Bognor. There was nothing for it but to head further out to sea, work to the eastward as much as we could and not tack back toward the shore until we were sure that we were clear of danger. A new complication arose when the boat began to roll at the precise rate which would set the compass rotating. It was exactly like swirling a bowl of water around in your hands. The liquid in the compass bowl rotated, the compass card rotated with it, and there was no way of checking our direction any more. Of course I could maintain the same angle with wind and sea, but if the wind continued to change direction we would become hopelessly lost.

Things really couldn't be said to be improving. Constant spray, and sometimes larger lumps of sea, gradually soaked my clothing inside my oilskins. Down below things were none too good either. Bob, feeling steadily worse, was lying on the floorboards with his head resting on my steel toolbox. He didn't seem aware that it was uncomfortable. We were taking in some water through the seams now that the seas were pounding and twisting our hull. Water was swilling across the floor around Bob's feet. After a while it began to hail. I made up some orange squash; we didn't have a swinging frame for the galley stove then, so I couldn't boil a kettle until things calmed down a bit. Unfortunately salt water had got into the tank and it tasted filthy. Poor Bob swallowed some before I realised what had happened. It did him no good at all. Not until long afterward did I realise that the pollution was only in the outlet pipe, not the tank itself. If we had run off another pint we could have had 30 gallons of good fresh water to drink; but we didn't know that and we had nothing more to drink that day.

At long last a watery sun appeared, the clouds thinned and the sea quieted a little. We headed in toward where land ought to be; Bob, by some superhuman effort, overcoming his misery and coming out to the cockpit. We saw land. It was a part of Sussex which I have known since childhood but I had great difficulty in identifying it from seaward. Finally we were convinced. We were well past Worthing and must double back on our course. Night would soon fall, we had missed our tide and could not hope to enter the Arun until at least 2 a.m. The shallows off Littlehampton extend for about four miles, so we would have to anchor that far off and wait. The wind shifted to the north and began to rise again as we made our way back along the coast. There are no outlying dangers in that area, so we could keep the shore lights in view. I watched the twinkling strands of the street lamps, stretching away to the distant glow which was Brighton, and thought of warmth, comfort and ease, as I shivered in my wet clothing. So far we were sheltered from the worst of the wind, now blowing from the shore. As we neared Littlehampton and were obliged to move further out to sea to avoid the shallows, its full force began to be felt. Short, steep waves formed and more spray swept over the decks. We anchored, finally, abeam of the point where the street lamps gave way to the dark stretch of the sand dunes which lead toward Bognor Regis.

Both bilge pumps had by now jammed with rubbish dislodged by our violent motion. The hoses were clear; the problems were inside the pumps themselves and this was no time to try dismantling them. We took a bucket. raised the floorboards and began to bail. The level quickly fell and it was soon obvious that, now that we were no longer smashing into the seas, no more was coming in. We had anchored at about 10.30 p.m. By midnight the bilges were empty, we had changed into dry clothing, the alarm clock was set for 2.30 a.m. and we were in our bunks.

We awoke to a violent rolling motion which made getting into our oilskins an acrobatic feat. At one point I was thrown completely over the saloon table, fortunately so muffled and padded by clothing that I came to no harm. Out in the cockpit we huddled down out of the force of the wind and discussed our tactics for getting underway. Bob, always at his best in a difficult situation, offered to go forward onto the foredeck alone and raise the anchor. Although he is much stronger than me I doubted if he could stay on his feet and pull in chain at the same time, under those conditions; but once the anchor broke free it would be essential to keep the bows from blowing round and bringing the breaking waves on to our beam, or we should be swamped. I would have to use the motor to ease the strain on the anchor chain and judge the exact moment to go ahead as the anchor broke free. Too soon and I would tighten the chain, dragging it from Bob's hands, perhaps injuring him. Too late and we would fall off broadside to the weather, making it impossible to lift and secure the anchor and perhaps sweeping Bob overboard. It was a pitch black night, made more so by the distant shore lights which prevented our night vision from developing.

The motor thudded reassuringly under my feet. We would be driving dead into wind, so the sails could be of no help to us. Bob disappeared, moving crabwise past the dinghy on deck into the blackness forward, keeping low to avoid the force of the wind. I waited anxiously, trying to judge by feel alone when the bows began to swing free; edging gently forward to reduce the tension on the chain. We seemed to begin turning. Opening the throttle wide I pushed the tiller over to keep us heading for the shore. To my great relief Bob reappeared calmly from the darkness, quite unconcerned by the difficult and dangerous job which he had just done. We peered into the darkness, trying to make out the entrance lights against the much brighter background of the street lamps. Fortunately that is something which I am quite good at, because it is by no means an unusual problem. Soon we were forging toward the river mouth, where smooth water at last gave us some respite. The wind also was screened by the buildings along the waterside. We came cautiously alongside the Bevis wharf, tied up and went ashore to telephone the news of our safe arrival to Vicki. Ice glittered in the gutters and cold blasts of air whined and moaned in the streets.

The next morning dawned clear and sunny. The wharf was coated in frost but smoke from a pile of burning scrap wood rose vertically into the air. John, already at work on the quayside as I poked my head out of the hatch, called a cheerful greeting. I cooked a good breakfast, brewed coffee and coaxed Bob out of his bunk. We tidied up, explained to John and Andy the reason for our delayed arrival and set out for home and hot baths. It was the last time we were to sail for almost two years, though we were unaware of it then.

What we now envisaged was lifting the boat out of the water, carrying out the surveyor's recommendations, doing a few modifications to our own requirements, storing and setting off. We were running a little late on our original timetable, but we still expected to leave that summer. We first had to remove the four tons of inside ballast, partly to reduce the load on the yard crane, but also to avoid straining the hull when it was lifted. Our eldest daughter, Catherine, then nine years old, came with me on my next visit to Littlehampton and looked after me so that I could concentrate my efforts entirely on lifting blocks of cast iron.

The tidal rise there is considerable, indeed we rested entirely on the mud for several hours out of each twelve. So the ballast removal had to be carried out quickly during a period of about two hours whilst the top of the quay was within arms reach from the deck. Each block of cast iron, weighing half a hundredweight and "T" shaped to fit between the frames of the hull, had to be levered clear of its neighbour, gripped in the fingertips, dragged from beneath floor level, carried up the companion steps to the deck, then lifted across to the quay. We managed to get half of it out during the first afternoon, then, by getting up at 3 a.m. I removed the rest at the next high water. Most of Sunday was taken up with carrying it across the quay and stacking it out of the way. Later Bob undertook the task of removing the loose rust with a wire brush, a filthy and tiring job, after which we repainted them all with black tar varnish.

By the next time we arrived John and Andy had craned "Dorothy Ann" up onto the quay. She looked enormous, occupying the entire space and still overhanging the river by several feet. With great ingenuity and skill they then built a wheeled steel cradle beneath the hull, strong enough to support it upright, and somehow manhandled this monstrous load through the doors into the boat shed.

Once there, we began work. The ballast had been simply resting on the hull framework under its own weight; if the boat was rolled over too far under extreme conditions it could be thrown about, endangering the stability and possibly causing damage and injury. A first priority then was to secure it, and this we proposed to do by bolting straps made of steel angle across the hull at every frame. To do this we needed to get at the frames and it was that which caused a major delay. We discovered that all the bulkheads and cabin furniture had been built by a gradual process of addition using, say, the end of a chest of drawers to support the upper half of a bulkhead and the end of a bunk. The result was that as soon as we wanted to move a bunk, for instance, to get at the space beneath, the next piece of the interior collapsed. As we also needed to rebuild all the lockers, which were quite inadequate for the huge amount of stowage needed for a long voyage, we realised that we might as well strip the interior completely and start again. It was a good decision, which we never regretted, but it enormously increased our work load.

Another task was to add a substantial oak band around the outside of the hull. There was no telling what wharves or other vessels we might have to lie alongside during the course of our travels, indeed this proved in practice to be a great factor in our peace of mind, protecting our planking from damage on innumerable occasions. Andy, who specialised in obtaining good boat building timber, managed to find us a supply of suitable planks at a very reasonable price. These, I decided, would be a lot easier to attach to the curve of the hull if we could put a bend in them first. I supported them off the ground at one end, piled on to them as much as I could of the contents of the boat and left gravity to do the rest. We were busy with other things for the next few weekends, but Bob managed to visit the yard for some purpose in our absence. On his return he telephoned us to say that I had stacked the oak planks carelessly, so that they had become warped. He, however, had fortunately spotted this, turned them over and weighted them down to straighten them. It would be difficult to say which of us was the more embarrassed when I explained.

Even with the workload which we had, we still hoped to leave that year. Andy had other ideas though. "Look" he said, "your first priority must be to refasten the hull." We knew he was right. It was something which "Stormy"

Davies had said we should consider, even before we bought "Dorothy Ann". She was fastened together by iron spikes driven through her planks into the oak frames, a cheap but strong method of work boat construction common at the time when she was built. Iron rusts however, especially in the presence of sea water, and she was over 40 years old. There was ample space to add a new pair of spikes diagonally opposite the old ones on each frame. Thus we would be sure that the hull would have even greater strength than originally, since the strength of a planked hull is determined by the strength of its fastenings and obviously most of the original ones were still strong enough to hold it together.

"Then" said Andy, "you had better completely recaulk the seams and you can be confident in the worst weather that the hull is sound." He was so obviously right and so honestly concerned for our safety that we decided at once to take his advice. He and John obtained our materials, taught us how to do the job and helped us when we were flagging. There was no charge for all this, even though the business was struggling to survive. First and foremost both partners loved wooden boats.

There was far too much to do now for us to have any hope of leaving as planned. We were all still doing full time jobs, increased mortgage rates had resulted in a complete lack of house buyers and clearly nothing could be settled for another year. We changed our planned leaving date to April 1982 and settled down to a long slog. To work effectively we needed to stay overnight in Littlehampton at weekends and holidays, but because of insurance regulations we could not sleep aboard "Dorothy Ann" whilst she was in the yard. In any case, we had taken out all of the interior. We decided that a motor caravan would be the answer. I had sold my car and begun cycling to work, partly as an economy measure but mostly to toughen me up a little for the forthcoming voyage. We had, therefore a small sum of money available. What could we get for it?

The answer was "the van". Unlike any of our other vehicles that was the only name it ever had, although

Vicki often used several adjectives in front of it, as in "That ⋆!%%XXX@?: van" or, more often, "YOUR ⋆%£@$ van." It really served us rather well. Most of the trouble was caused by her first unfortunate experience of it. We bought it from an Australian girl who, with her mother, had taken it from England to Switzerland and back. How they managed it I shall never know, but it had a wheel on each corner and the engine started. I doubted if we could expect much more for what we could afford to pay. We drove down in Vicki's car, paid for the van and started it up. Vicki climbed in and drove it out of the driveway. I thought she would stop in the road outside, but she drove away into the darkness.

What followed would have been good material for an old silent film comedy. I, wanting to keep up with her in case of problems, jumped quickly into her car and drove off after her. She was nowhere in sight when I reached the main road, nor could I find her when I drove in a complete circuit around the area. Well, she must be somewhere on the road home to Wokingham and surely it couldn't take long for her Alfa Romeo to catch up with the lumbering van! I raced into nearby Basingstoke only to see the van crossing ahead of me at traffic lights. Attempting to follow, after the lights changed, I found myself caught up in an unfamiliar one way system. Eventually I saw her ahead again, but once again I was stopped by the traffic lights. Finally, several miles further on, I managed to catch up with her. She was travelling surprisingly quickly up a viciously winding road and I found I needed all the Alfa's excellent cornering ability just to keep up with her. How she was keeping the van on the road was a mystery.

By some miracle we arrived home unscathed and I was immediately in trouble. I must be out of my mind! How could I have bought such a piece of wreckage? And far more words to that effect. It turned out that she had only set out to drive round the block and check out the vehicle, and furthermore she had returned to say that it was worthless and to tell me to demand my money back. By then, of course, I had chased off to look for her and she thought that I had driven home without waiting for her. The reason for her speed on the way home was that the van had a tendency to stall altogether if she allowed it to slow down. It would probably have overturned, but the tyres were so completely bald that the back wheels tended to lose adhesion and slide easily around all the bends. It also had a long and sloppy gear lever which caused her to smash her hand on the metal dashboard every time she changed into third gear. I was not exactly popular.

It was basically the smallest model of Commer van, with a pop up roof extension and some rudimentary furnishings. The table could be lowered level with the seats to form a double bed, there was a bunk about four feet long at the rear, a sink, a cooker and a couple of cupboards. Fitting five of us into it was an interesting exercise and useful experience in conserving space, something which was even more necessary aboard "Dorothy Ann". Our scheme was for Vicki, Catherine and myself to squeeze into the double bed and put Hilary who, at five years old, was still quite small, on the short bunk at the rear. That left seven year old Diana. We found that, with care, she could be slid, in her sleeping bag, into the space between the seats, under our double bed.

Another major source of problems, and one which was never dealt with satisfactorily, was the decks. Probably the only sensible way to make a caulked deck properly waterproof is to strip it of all fittings, sand it completely smooth and glue a layer of marine plywood completely over it. It is a tremendous amount of work and bother, as any flaw in the work will allow water to penetrate and cause disastrous rot in the structure beneath. Properly done though, it is totally watertight and adds immense strength to the boat. We already had enough to do though, and thought that an adequate job could be done by coating the decks with a well known synthetic resin based covering, sold for that purpose, which we knew from past experience to be a good product. It was a pity really that Vicki, telephoning the manufacturers late one day, with a technical query, got into conversation with their technical director.

"With what will you caulk it, dear Liza, dear Liza?" he said, or words to that effect. "Why not try our excellent polysulphide caulking? It's very effective and far cheaper than the American brands on the market." They sent us free samples, which we tried out. It seemed to be very good, easy to apply, adhering well to the wood and having the elasticity to allow for the shrinking and swelling of the planks which occurs constantly. We removed all the putty from the decks and replaced it with this "superior" product. "We will use this on the underwater hull" we said. It was Andy who saved us from total disaster. "I'm sure it's an excellent product" he said diplomatically, "but we've been using red lead putty for an awfully long time now and we're certain that it works. I really think you shouldn't risk trying out a new method below the waterline in a boat which is going offshore." It was several weeks before we found out how right he was.

Vicki was working high up among the roof girders as I prepared the hull for the new fastenings. A boat out of the water always looks very tall, especially when it is raised up on a cradle. In this case the deck was about 12 feet above the ground, so that Vicki was forced to crawl and stoop among a forest of rusty metal, suffering many a bruise and graze as she worked. For weeks she toiled to dig out putty and remove old paint from the decks. Then there was the new caulking compound to apply over the cotton. Luckily for us the manufacturers said that cotton, though not really necessary with their product, should be used simply to reduce the space to be filled and save on the amount of the polysulphide needed. Finally she applied two thick coats of the resin based deck covering compound, following the instructions for its use carefully.

Happy that the decks would be sound and dry, we could now confidently tackle the interior rebuilding. "Dorothy Ann" could not stay under cover for too long; her planks would dry out, shrink and crack, loosening the caulking and causing leaks. Soon she must go back into the river and take whatever weather came her way. I had by now drilled the 1,350 complex, stepped diameter holes, which were necessary to allow the new fastenings to be driven through into the iron hard oak frames, without splitting the wood and with the heads sunk well below the outer surface of the planks. I began the task of driving in the new spikes and Vicki began raking out the old caulking from the underwater seams, ready to recaulk as soon as the new fastenings were all in.

Of course, we didn't really do each job neatly, one after the other as I have described them. Often there were frustrating delays. Materials were not available, demands on our time clashed. We would both pitch in together when the start of the next job depended on the completion of the last. Sometimes we would alternate between two or more jobs just to avoid monotony. Tools broke, or were left at home. Access to parts of the hull was impeded by other boats and jobs as work went on around us in the shed. Sometimes we would despair. Then Stuart, our neighbour in the shed, would cheer us up. He was a master carpenter and shipwright, whose tremendous skill put us to shame. He had bought a single log, an entire tree trunk of beautiful, hard iroko wood, sawn it up, and was now building, of all things, an Eventide. When we despaired of one of our efforts, thinking how amateurish it looked compared with Stuart's beautiful craftsmanship, he would just smile and say "Step back a bit, all boatbuilding looks perfect from 20 feet away." As time went on we realised that he, too, had his failures, but when things went wrong he would calmly begin again and, quite quickly it seemed to us, he would get the job done properly.

Our first journey down to Littlehampton in the van was quite uneventful. When we started it up at about 7.30 p.m. to leave the boatyard after our day's work however, the oil pressure warning lamp remained lit. We switched off hastily and checked the oil level, sure enough, it was very low. Everyone had gone home; the wind sighed dismally down the dark streets and we had no idea where there might be a filling station open that late. A small seaside town in winter hardly abounds in evening trade and most businesses are firmly closed by 6 p.m. I tried a short foray on foot, but soon became discouraged and we resigned ourselves to spending the night where we were. The small parking space outside the yard doors had a pronounced slope downward into the road, causing us to continually slide in a heap to the bottom of our bed. We felt some alarm too as the noisy Saturday night pub crowds sang and swore their way home past us at 11 o'clock, but we remained unmolested. Morning came at last and the ever resourceful Andy telephoned a friend with a motor accessory business to deliver a gallon can of oil to the yard. From then on we kept a careful check on the level, making sure always to have a reserve of oil available in the van.

The task of wrapping the oak rubbing band around the hull, to protect us from the hard edges of wharves and other boats, continued over a long period. It was easier to coax the hard oak to the curve of the hull a little at a time and would, in the long run, make a better job of it than trying to force it into place all at once. Sometimes it felt as if nothing would ever be finished though. The yard, like any other boatyard, contained large power saws, planing equipment and other machinery. The children, though not banned from coming into the shed to speak to us, were naturally not allowed to play inside, where they would be a danger to themselves and to others. As a result, they spent long hours in the van. Used to the cramped conditions of small boats, which they had sailed in all their lives, they had an enormous capability to create their own amusements. One day, Vicki, seized by a pang of conscience, went out to see if they were O.K. "Don't disturb us now please," they said, "we're exploring Africa." This in a space about twelve feet by five, mostly impeded by furniture!

As the warmer weather brought the start of the sailing season, one boat owner, with a mooring just astern of ours, was so impressed by their ingenuity and good behaviour that he invited them to sail with him at the weekends. So as we worked through the long, hot summer after shivering through the cold, clammy winter preceding it, they sailed with Peter to Bognor Regis and Brighton, up and down the sparkling Channel, sometimes returning late, tired, but happy, after missing their tide over the bar. Thus virtue brought its reward, whilst we worked endlessly on with all thoughts of sailing forced out of our minds. On other evenings, when we would drive the van up to the beach, on the opposite bank of the river where the golf course led up to sand dunes and a long stretch of beach unspoiled by buildings of any kind, Vicki and I would have the energy only to light the gas under our prepared supper, eat and fall into bed exhausted. The children though would disappear screaming with delight, armed with towels and swimming costumes, across the deserted beach to plunge into a leaden and chilly sea.

A couple of weeks after finishing the decks, Vicki had some reason to go up there and walk forward. As she trod on one of the seams the deck coating stuck to her shoe like chewing gum, pulling a great length of compound out of the seam and bringing the cotton out with it. Investigation soon showed that all the seams were in the same state. A frantic telephone call to the manufacturers went as follows:

"The deck covering is all dissolving and going sticky."

"Ah, it will be the plasticiser which keeps the caulking compound flexible doing that."

"We don't want to know what is doing it. What are you going to do about it?"

"Oh dear, we should have told you to put sealer in between. Never mind, we will send you some and some more materials free of charge and you can do it again."

How nice. Summer was beginning, "Dorothy Ann"s planks were beginning to dry rapidly as the temperature rose. We needed every minute to finish the repainting, refastening and recaulking, so that she could go back in the water as soon as possible. Now a major job which we thought was safely completed had to be done again. It was a tedious business completely stripping the decks again, made worse by the fact that much of the "new" compound was discovered to have gone hard in the tubes, blocking the nozzles repeatedly and making a filthy mess where the smaller lumps had to be removed from the seams to get a smooth unbroken finish. The job took three times as long as it would have if the compound had flowed smoothly as it should. The only good thing about it was that we did have enough tubes of compound to do the job, just, despite the wastage.

It was hot, dusty and cramped working high in the roof. Vicki took many a hard knock from the roof girders, the massive arms of a lifting gantry which was parked over the boat and sundry odd protrusions. She did the whole job singlehanded as I toiled frantically at other tasks below. There was no hope now of rebuilding the interior in the relative comfort and convenience of the yard. Bob came down for a few days, we painted frantically, then we were ready for the water again. The crane which had been used to lift us out had stripped its gears lifting a fishing boat and was not worth repairing. We discussed various options, finally deciding that, after so much work, it was foolish to take any cut price options. Accordingly we summoned an enormous, gleaming, travelling crane, capable of lifting the entire boat shed and all its contents if need be. Naturally this paragon was in great demand. We would have to wait until it was convenient for it to come to us.

By this time Ross and Margaret had returned, fit, bronzed and healthy, with enough funds to continue their journey. We collected them from Heathrow for a weekend together, after which they returned to Benfleet, quickly readied "Girl Morgan" for sea and set off once more. We saw them again, briefly, at the Eventide Owners Association meet, at Bradwell, on the Blackwater river in Essex; the first such meet we had attended without a boat of our own. Then they set off southward for the English Channel, on the first leg of their onward journey. The next news we received of them was that they had motored into a loose length of floating rope off the port of Newhaven, in Sussex. This rope, winding tightly around the propeller shaft, had pulled off the rear end of the gearbox, completely immobilising them as there was no wind at the time. They had been very lucky to attract the attention of a passing vessel which towed them safely into Newhaven.

This news reached us at Littlehampton one weekend when we could do little more before the crane arrived. Accordingly we set out in the van for Newhaven to give what help we could, despite a rather ominous trickle of fluid oozing from one of the brake drums. It was a really pleasant summer's day, attracting a plentiful stream of traffic to the coast road. Soon my right arm was aching as the brakes, in frequent use, pulled ever more violently to the right. We reached Newhaven without mishap however and were in time to be of some help in dragging the heavy Volvo engine in "Girl Morgan" out of its seating, ready for repair. Their youngest son Colin was with them on this occasion and the eight of us had a very pleasant time together, until it was time for us to make our way, rather late at night, back to Wokingham. The traffic was very light by then, so I was able to drive easily with a minimum of braking, the children tucked into their beds in the back, arriving home in the small hours without incident.

5
Setbacks

I forget now the reason why I could not get to Littlehampton on "Crane day". It may have been work or possibly a disabling rheumatic pain in my leg which gave me a lot of trouble that year. Whatever the reason it was poor Bob who was given the unwelcome responsibility of being our "Man on the Spot". The crane driver was a man who thought big. He simply had "Dorothy Ann" brought out into the street in front of the yard, lifted her up, carried her a few yards clear of obstructions, then lifted all eight tons of her to a height of about 30 feet, clean over the rooftops, to lower her neatly and gently into the river. Bob, helpless to do much except watch and take photographs, was horrified when, at the highest point, "Dorothy Ann" slipped a fraction in her slings, but soon he was scrambling aboard to check the hull for leaks.

And leaks there were aplenty, for had the caulking been driven home too tightly the cotton could swell with enough force to cause more harm than good. Under Andy's careful tuition though, we had got it just right and within minutes it had slowed to a trickle, then dried altogether. From then on we could always leave her for weeks if we wished, without taking in a drop of water. Of course, if we really drove her hard to windward she would begin to leak a little, as any planked boat must, but as soon as sail was reduced or the boat turned to bring the weather further aft there would be no further need to pump. It was still to be quite a time though before we were at all concerned with what happened at sea. We had the whole of the interior to rebuild, after first replacing the ballast and fitting its retaining straps; no easy task in itself. The masts had to be oiled and replaced, all the standing and running rigging attached, electrical equipment, instruments and wiring fitted. We were also going to rebuild the cockpit, making it and the lockers in it completely watertight, then fitting drains and seacocks.

We had a buyer for the house at last, but at a very disappointing price. We would be selling for no more than the actual price we had paid two years before, which in those days of rampant inflation meant a loss in real terms. Also the company for which I had worked for the last 15 years was about to make substantial numbers of people redundant. They were hardly likely to look kindly on the idea of staff taking extended leaves, even unpaid ones, when 5,000 people were about to lose their jobs altogether. So rather than try to avoid redundancy I opted to take a modest but useful severance payment, which was about the amount we had hoped to make on the house when we first did our calculations.

We continued to travel to and fro to Littlehampton on most weekends, and on one Sunday evening the van decided to make another bid for our attention. Apart from the high oil consumption, which we had learned to live with, and the braking problem, which we had cured, it had given no trouble. That evening however, as we rolled out of a filling station about 15 miles before reaching home, there came a loud bang, followed almost at once by another, and the gear lever jammed solid. We coasted across the road and came to a halt. As usual, it was getting late, in fact even as we sat wondering what on earth could have happened, the lights of the filling station went out as it closed down for the night.

I crawled under the van and groped for the long arm which connected the lever with the actual gearbox. The arm itself was jammed solid, how I could not imagine but clearly it was not something I was likely to fix lying in the road in the dark. I wrenched hard at it, trying to dislodge whatever was jamming it; I shudder now at the thought of what would have happened if I had succeeded. We decided that I would set off toward Wokingham on foot and try to get a lift home. Then I could drive Vicki's car back and tow the van home to where we could repair it more easily. We certainly didn't have the money to pay for towage or repair.

I set off, not too optimistically, along the deserted road. A car passed by on the other side. Nothing at all in my direction. A little time passed. I walked stoically onward, wondering how long it would be before I got to bed. It had, as usual, been a long, tiring weekend and I had a great deal of work awaiting me on Monday morning; this morning, it soon would be, I mused. Then a solitary car appeared behind me. It seemed to be travelling fairly slowly, perhaps the driver was looking for a particular address. It drew alongside, the driver leaning across toward me. Doubtless, as I was a relative stranger to the area, he was going to ask for directions. But no. He was a good samaritan who had seen the van apparently in trouble and returned, after driving his girl friend home, to offer help. After speaking to Vicki and finding out the problem, he had driven on to find me.He even had a tow rope, albeit a little short, a rather daunting thing in a vehicle with the driving seat set right at the front, so that you feel right on top of the towing vehicle. More of a problem though was the fact that his car had a slightly slipping clutch, so that it was necessary to keep the speed up, particularly when approaching and climbing hills.

We set out, therefore, at a fair clip, Vicki riding in the car ahead to give directions, myself and the three girls, now wide awake and interested, rolling and swaying behind in eerie silence. It was a dark and winding route, no easy motorway driving, and twice the rope broke when we took up the slack with too great a jerk. Suddenly Diana said:

"Daddy, I feel sick."

"Well, there isn't a lot I can do about it," I replied; we were hurtling up a particularly dark and twisting stretch at the time, the road turning, dipping and rising again, needing every bit of my attention to keep an even tension on the rope. There was no way I was going to voluntarily stop and restart there, it was narrow and dangerous and we were likely to have the devil of a job getting started again. So she was. And we just had to live with it. If only we had known the danger we were in we would probably not even have noticed that; as it was, my concentration then was all on the car so close ahead of me, on the need to react instantly if he should need to brake hard, so I just hastily opened the window and kept my mind on the task in hand.

Amazingly, as it now seems, we reached Wokingham safely. Our new found friend accepted a cup of coffee and was persuaded, with some reluctance, to accept the cost of his petrol for the journey. He didn't stay long, he was already going to be quite late home; so we were in our beds not long after midnight despite our mishap.

We had towed, and been towed in, quite a few vehicles over the years, so there was nothing very special about that. It was only on the following Saturday, when I at last had time to examine the vehicle closely, that our extraordinary good fortune became evident. The first bang we had heard had been caused by one of the right hand front suspension bolts shearing in half. The second had been its companion, unable to take the double load, following suit. The suspension arm had then been no longer attatched at the top at all and, had it not accidentally jammed on the gear lever extension rod, the front wheel would have been free to fall outward onto its side. Had I succeeded in wrenching it free from below, the vehicle would have fallen on me. Had we hit a slightly larger bump (there were quite a few) on the way home, the wheel would have collapsed and we would probably have gone off the road, very likely overturning in the process. Sometimes people ask how we can risk the dangers of going to sea; I'm not at all sure that there are many dangers compared with life on land, it is just that people have learned to live with the everyday ones by ignoring them or pretending that they don't exist.

We had not had "Dorothy Ann" back on the water long when we noticed the tell tale softening of the deck coating over the seams once more. We really had enough to do, trying to build bulkheads, bunks, lockers and galley, without that job again, but it could not be ignored. Back to the telephone:

"Goodness how strange! What sealer did we send you?"

Vicki fetched the can and read off the number.

"Oh dear, what a shame, we seem to have sent the wrong one. We will just have to send you some more of everything..........!"

It had been suggested, after our previous trouble, that the Technical Director would be willing to come down and investigate any further problem. Vicki mentioned this:

"Oh yes he would be glad to, only he has just been called away indefinitely; to Nigeria."

We did it all again; this time I helped a good deal, just to preserve Vicki's sanity. We collected old net curtains from our friends, tore them into strips, soaked them liberally in the new sealer and plastered them over the newly caulked seams with many more coats of sealer. Finally we painted on the new deck coating. It was water soluble until it had cured, just like emulsion paint. We had torrential rain, just before it could set, which washed it all off the decks and over the oiled topsides, where it promptly set in ugly runs and streaks. At this point we received a gay little letter from the manufacturer's publicity department, saying that they were publicising the fact that their products were being successfully used on our seagoing yacht. It is probably a good thing I was too busy to reply.

We were treating all unpainted woodwork with an extremely expensive, but allegedly superior oil finish, in the belief that it would afford better protection to the wood than the more usual varnish, and maintain a better appearance. The instructions were to apply at least 25 coats to the wood before allowing the surface to dry, but allowing sufficient time between coats for the oil to soak in. Vicki, once again, claimed this job, as she is usually responsible for all aspects of the appearance of our possessions, my job being simply to make them work. She lined up sufficient work to ensure that applying one coat to all the pieces took long enough for the first to be ready for its next coat as she finished the last. She then applied oil for about 10 hours, non stop. The oil was thin, designed to penetrate easily into the wood grain; naturally it penetrated clothing just as effectively and, as it was impossible to work in the cramped corner where the masts were stored on trestles without coming into contact with the oiled surfaces, especially when working at speed, poor Vicki was saturated to the skin and even her underclothes were fit only for the rag bag. That was another sacrifice made in vain. The oil, despite its exotic Scandinavian name, proved to be another triumph of advertising over reality. It weathered out of the wood at unbelievable speed, whereas the old varnish on the mizen crutches, which we overlooked and then couldn't find time to do, was still intact when we reached Australia.

How much of the money and time wasted on the inferior products of lying manufacturers, or, more accurately, their advertisers, could we have devoted to more safety features, which might have saved our boat when things went wrong? We shall never know, but my dislike of a lot of advertising claims, always quite strong, has increased considerably. How I wish advertisers were liable to the sort of prosecution and stupefying damages which are regularly inflicted on perfectly honest citizens in the U.S.A. for the slightest accidental slip, error or often simple mischance in the practice of their professions. But, even in that country, advertisers bear no responsibility at all.

It wasn't just materials. Rather than try to cut corners by buying secondhand, we bought a brand new sewing machine of a type allegedly built for the express purpose of sail repairs and claiming to be suitable for use on board small boats. Even Clare Francis, whom we all admire greatly, lent her name in praise of the damn thing. Another good reason why we should try to avoid sponsorship. For it was bloody useless. There is no polite adjective adequate to describe it. It never sewed a single seam without some fault and in a salt atmosphere it instantly rusted so badly that it always took at least three hours of cleaning and polishing to get it to work at all. It never would penetrate more than two thicknesses of cloth either, so the corners of sails, which take most of the wear and are reinforced by several layers, always had to be repaired by hand anyway.

The electric automatic helming device which failed after less than four hours' use was a similar product, widely touted as having steered some vast number of racing yachts around the world. Doubtless they had, but only because the manufacturers presumably flew infinite numbers of free replacements for them to each port, I suspect. This particular piece of garbage did however provide us with an amusing tale in Auckland, which I will relate in its proper place. A further problem in fitting out for a long voyage is that, obviously, everything cannot be done at once. This means that some items of equipment are bought well before departure, particularly as the complexity of the project is most likely to result in some delay to the original plans. So by the time they fail, just out of sight of land on the first leg of the voyage, they are safely out of warranty. Of course it is inadvisable to name the people who have caused us so much trouble and needless expense. The law protects them far more from our valid criticism than us from their deceit. It is possible though, and a great pleasure also, to give credit to the Poole based company, Electronic Laboratories, whose cheap yet effective "Seafarer" and "Seafix" instruments served us far better than any other. They also corrected a fault on an instrument on which the warranty had expired, free of charge, when I wrote explaining the delay between purchase and use. I commend them to sailors everywhere.

Eventually we finished the decks again, and this time they remained hard and leakproof. We really thought that was the end of that problem. I had set up a sawbench on top of the ballast in the area which was to become the saloon and, despite the problems caused by having to carry materials such as eight by four foot sheets of plywood down a 20 foot vertical ladder and working with the boat tilted sideways at an angle of 25 degrees at low water twice a day, progress was being made. The anchor windlass had been taken home to be stripped, given new bearings and have its casing re-galvanised. The four tons of ballast were laboriously replaced. The ballast straps, also galvanised, by one of Andy's endless list of useful contacts, were now clamped firmly to the frames, holding the ballast tightly in place.

Large numbers of farewell parties were being held in the various divisions of the company for which I worked, as we who were redundant prepared to go our separate ways. This offered some opportunity to enjoy life whilst pursuing the main objective and at one of these parties, held at a Reading pub, another diversion came our way. Peter, who had worked for one of my colleagues, was moving to a job in the Stockport area. Not having a driver's licence himself he asked me, carefully choosing a moment when I might be supposed to be in a convivial mood, whether I would drive a rental truck containing his belongings up to his new home. I explained that we could do better than that. The van ought to be quite capable of doing that job, so he could save the cost of the rental and need only pay for fuel.

In due course we loaded the van with his worldly goods, which were, of course, far greater in volume than he had realised. However, we got them all in, leaving space for one adult and the three children to lie down in the back. By bolting an old swivel chair top on to the engine cover we were able to seat three adults in the front and so we set off, on a Saturday evening; Peter in the passenger seat, his girl friend, Sue, on top of the engine, myself driving and Vicki and our three girls in the back. Vicki and I, of course, were practising watch keeping, driving for three hours each and sleeping alternately in between. We had an uneventful trip, saw Peter into his new flat by midday on Sunday and drove home via Jodrell Bank, with its great radio telescope, the vale of Evesham, where ripe fruit was on sale from innumerable roadside stands, and Oxford; arriving back at Wokingham on Sunday evening. A nice break from boatbuilding. Probably Sue is the only girl ever to have travelled from Reading to Stockport in a typist's chair.

Although our house was about to be sold at last, and "Geisha" had finally found a buyer, enabling us to clear our debt to the bank, our original plan needed some modification. Bob was going to have to keep working until just before we left, in order to have any cash for the trip. So he would need to keep his house in Tiptree and we could expect a long delay in selling that also. We therefore abandoned the plan of buying a new property near the boat, deciding instead to buy part of Bob's house and relieve him of the need to make mortgage repayments. We could store our furniture there, but needed a base in Littlehampton. The answer was to rent a holiday house for the winter, at a low rate. By the time of the first summer holiday bookings we would, we thought, be long gone. We used a removal truck to take the large furniture to Tiptree, but the van carried the rest of our possessions to Littlehampton. Its purpose fulfilled, we sold it shortly afterward. Despite its faults it had given us good service for a capital cost of under £200.

I began to work full time on the boat, the children settled down happily at their new school, Vicki tried to find a job locally to support us but, although she still had her car and could have commuted a reasonable distance, there was nothing to be had. Probably just as well, as she had plenty to do for the voyage, but it meant spending more of our small capital just on everyday expenses. I began a routine of rising at 6 a.m. (not my favourite time) and doing half an hour of Canadian Air Force exercises, a routine allegedly promoting physical well being. I would then have breakfast and leave for the yard at 7 o'clock, taking a sandwich lunch. And there, until the yard closed at 6 p.m. (yes, even John and Andy were cutting down their working hours) I would remain. Actually, since I was working on the boat herself, only needing the shed for storing materials and prefabricating some jobs, I could go on later if need be, but usually it seemed a long enough day. I tried to take Sundays off, or at least to work in the garage at the house.

Work went ahead steadily, if rather more slowly than I

had hoped. The Sussex coast usually has mild winters, as I had found to my disgust when as a schoolboy I had waited for the snow to arrive each winter, only to discover that it seldom covered the top of the grass. It freezes though, and even several degrees above freezing, resin glues lose interest in hardening. It was frustrating to remove the clamps from a job which had been glued three days before and have it fall apart, despite all attempts to heat the interior of the boat; especially as the same Resorcinol glue set solid in about 10 minutes in summer, usually before the job could be properly assembled. If only I had known of the far more tractable Epoxy glues which are the only ones approved for boatbuilding in New Zealand; but that was a long way in the future.

Christmas came and went and the snow, now that I could have happily done without it, arrived in generous quantities. I have always been prone to odd rheumatic pains, in randomly selected limbs, and now my right leg, aggravated by a fall in the snow, began to give trouble. It was too slippery to use the bike any more, so I had to limp, irritably, the half mile or so to the boatyard each day. We did feel though that this sort of thing confirmed our wisdom in trying to do something a bit out of the ordinary now, rather than waiting for retirement and then being frustrated by infirmity perhaps. We just kept on trying to do our best.

One black and howling night I turned out, after a phone call from Andy, to put extra stern lines on "Dorothy Ann". A blizzard was driving snow directly up the river and piling up a strong flood tide. All the boats were straining at their lines, the black water rising to lift them high above the quay. For a while I feared that the canvas cover which we had rigged completely over "Dorothy Ann" to give protection from the elements would be torn away, but it held and after a while the tide turned, countering the force of the wind against the hull and easing the strain on the lines. It was that winter's last really unpleasant spell. We worked on, gradually making progress. Spring came at last, bringing floods which flowed over the quay and across the boat shed floor but luckily stopped short of floating the boats right up onto the quay. That had once happened in Paris, to a barge owned by Vicki's parents, so we were aware of the problems and dangers of ultra high tides and hovered nervously on the quay when one was predicted.

By March the six bunks, three in the fo'c's'le for the children; a double and a single between the fo'c's'le and the saloon for ourselves and Bob, were completed. The floorboards were not down yet, the sea toilet was not fitted, the galley stove was on deck under the canvas cover and the entire after end of the boat was still an empty shell. We had craned the masts back in, Vicki spending long hours high above rooftop level in a "bosun's chair", fitting the complete new set of standing and running rigging which she had obtained and spliced over the Christmas period. Every wire, rope, block and shackle was new. We were taking no chances with vital equipment. Then I fell ill.

A kidney infection, our doctor said. Take these pills, go to bed, rest, take it easy for a while! I spent a week in bed, growing daily more irritable. A vast quantity of stores arrived. Vicki and her friend Jackie toiled in the sitting room below me, packing it all in carefully calculated lots so that it could be stowed in an accessible manner. After I got up I dutifully spent a couple of days on the beach, well wrapped up, relaxing and doing nothing more strenuous than writing letters. I felt fine. Then I plunged back into the backlog of work. The following week I virtually collapsed and this time the pills didn't work. We had already extended the lease of the house by one month; it was fully booked for holidays from then on. Bob was now living with us most of the time, making occasional visits to Tiptree. The six of us moved aboard "Dorothy Ann".

A little while ago our friend Reese published a delightful and unusual book, called "Unlikely Passages". The book strays lightly over a wide range of the Author's sailing and personal experiences and should surely appeal to any genuine "blue water" sailor. I mention it here though because it was criticised by an American reviewer as being too much concerned with sex and bodily functions. Clearly he didn't know much about long passages in small boats. Equally clearly, Reese does. Sex we shall come to later; which, on reflection, may be an adequate summary of the subject, when one chooses a lifestyle which combines near exhaustion with total lack of privacy. The operation of the body, though usually unobtrusive and given about as much conscious attention as breathing, is a noticeable and critical phenomenon when engaged on a physically demanding activity in close proximity to other people. In health it can provide amusement, in an enjoyably vulgar way; sometimes irritation and annoyance. In sickness it becomes both a burden and a source of worry.

So, I was stuck on my bunk, not daring to do any work at all. Except of course that the sea toilet was not fitted, so my condition necessitated frequent trips out of bed, up onto the larger boat inshore of us, across that, up the vertical ladder on the wharf side (about 20 feet, at low water) across the quay and through the boat shed to the yard toilets. I shall be forever grateful for Bob's present to me for my 47th birthday; he installed the boat's loo! How we all managed to go on looking forward to the voyage in those circumstances is difficult to explain. It wasn't just fear of the shambles which would result if we gave up then which drove us, though that surely played a part. We simply weren't beaten yet, so there was no need to give up. Vicki cooked for the six of us on the paraffin stove on deck, crouching under the canvas cover. Bob, after installing the loo, got on with the electrical wiring and radio installation. The children crossed the next boat, climbed the ladder, went through the yard and walked to school each day. Our tolerant neighbour, Michael, stoically put up with the thunder of feet across his decks, spent hours amusing the children and let them watch his T.V.

I didn't get any better; all attempts to sneak back to work resulting in fever and exhaustion after an hour or so. "Have you" said my doctor, "been rather overdoing things?" It wasn't really a question, since she knew about our activities from our many visits for immunisation treatments. I took the hint, stopped trying to rush things and made myself relax completely. X-rays, complete with the delights of Barium meals and carried out despite a "Go slow" action by the Radiographers, showed nothing. We were unsure whether I was likely to die, spend my life attached to a machine, need some lesser medication, or simply recover. And no one was venturing an opinion. The only sensible thing was for everyone else to carry on doing what they could to prepare for the voyage, until I either got better or worse. Summer was now slipping rapidly by.

One remark which I was apt to repeat frequently was that anyone attempting to leave England in a small boat in October must be mentally unbalanced. The frequency and severity of gales in the English Channel and its Western Approaches makes it a virtual certainty that the boat will receive a severe mauling from the weather. The prevailing winds coming from ahead ensure that a fast passage during a favourable spell is almost impossible. A slow passage must hit bad weather. We had planned to leave in April, so as to have good conditions for the whole of the North Atlantic and Mediterranean passages; even if we were a little late in leaving, we should be well into the Eastern Mediterranean by autumn. But now?

The harsh truth was that we were too cramped and too broke to stay. Even if we could by some miracle remain sane and amicable until the spring, even if we could physically survive a whole winter in an unheated boat with no room to move below decks, our money would be dribbled away. We were not likely to find work locally, our cars were sold, so we could not travel easily; it would be difficult to be presentably turned out whilst living in our cramped conditions. The choice became: go now, or move ashore, with all that entailed in terms of cost and commitment, hoping to start again in the future. We discussed it anxiously; in the end there was only one conclusion possible, we must go when we were ready or give up altogether. And we weren't going to give up.

After an age I gingerly began to try again. Disciplining myself to no more than a few hours a day at first, I got back to work. Very slowly the saloon seats and lockers were completed. I felt fine, though a little weak. Soon I was working a full day again, though careful now not to try and go on for too long. Then the galley was finished and we had space to stow the stores which we had left in Jackie's garage for three weeks, six months ago! The six of us had also been making a twice weekly pilgrimage across Littlehampton to use Jackie's bath; we leaned heavily on her for physical and moral support and she gave freely of both. Other friends came to visit, knowing that it would be some years before we could meet again. We worked steadily on. Suddenly we realised that one more burst of maximum effort would see us able (ready is hardly the right word) to leave. It was October 12th, 1982.

Three days of frantic activity followed. We had on the quay an enormous pile of useful items ranging from old motor tyres, for fenders, to spare canvas and water containers, which we had scrounged or been given. The hardest task was to discard most of this heap, for there was far too little room to stow it aboard. As it was, quite a number of things ended up on the saloon floor, lashed to the table to keep them in place. On the evening of the third day (sounds very biblical, doesn't it?) we had done all we could.

"Now we will go," I said.

"But we can't leave tonight," said Bob and Vicki, "we are all exhausted." It was true. We had been working 16 or more hours a day for the past three days and were desperately tired. "But the weather is deteriorating" I said. "If we don't leave now we may be stuck here for ages." "Quite true," said Bob "but if we leave, we will be out in the Channel, exhausted, when the bad weather arrives." He was right; I agreed that we should get a good night's rest, and for three days we huddled miserably below as the gale which arrived next day blew viciously up the river, preventing us from leaving.

Surrounded by their books and possessions, Josh and Vicki are very much at home in "Dorothy Ann"

Josh and Catherine whiling away hot, lazy days on passage through the Red Sea

PART TWO DURING . . .

6
Setting Off

By the fourth morning the wind had died. Dawn broke to reveal smooth grey waters under a low overcast sky. There was no sense in hurrying our departure, we could afford the luxury of a leisurely breakfast as we waited for the tide to flood. Leaving at high water we would have no trouble crossing the bar and the ebb would carry us on our way to the westward. Slowly the tide rose and the stream slackened. The water along our sides became still. It was time to go. Michael came out onto the deck of "Floranda", alongside whom we had been moored for over a year. "Please let me cast off your lines," he asked politely, "I would like to have this small part in your voyage." We shook hands, thanking him for his tolerance and understanding during our time alongside. He cast off the lines then and we slipped rapidly away toward the river mouth.

We waved to the solitary figure of Ken, who had supplied our liferaft and waterproof clothing, sweeping up storm wrack outside his shop doorway, but I don't think he saw us. There were few other people about; none whom we knew. The ebbing tide and our thudding diesel engine took us on and out to sea, where we began to roll to the rise and fall of the restless waves. The wind was already rising again; this time from the west, exactly against us.

Not surprisingly, we made little progress beating down channel. We had planned ahead for this, as there is no point in struggling against a strong tide when anchorage is available. With a favourable wind we would press on ahead, but with this headwind the only sensible course was to make Bembridge Ledge, in the lee of the Isle of Wight, on this tide if possible, then lie there during the returning flood.

Bob, as usual, and the children, more surprisingly, were feeling very queasy. To our utter amazement, so was Vicki. This was hitherto unheard of, even on those Channel Ferries, operated by British Rail and apparently designed for the express purpose of causing their passengers to throw up. (As are, now that I think of it, many aspects of British Rail). As for me, I had decided long ago that if I wanted to skipper my own boat my stomach would have to do as it was told. It does, but I don't find life terribly enjoyable at such times.

Darkness came early and with it the new flood tide. We were heading toward our old friend the Nab tower; motoring now as there was little room to tack. We punched onward, wet and cold from rain and spray, looking forward to the smoother waters which we expected to find in the protection of the island. Past the Nab there was no noticeable improvement and we began to realise that, though it might be better than elsewhere, it was not going to be the peaceful anchorage which we had been longing for.

Once anchored our fears were confirmed. "Dorothy Ann" plunged and rolled dementedly on the end of her anchor warp. Eating was difficult, sleep impossible. I had put down our brand new Bruce anchor on a nylon warp, rather than using the heavy main C.Q.R. and chain, because I had only intended a short stay and wanted to avoid handling the heavy gear as much as possible. I now tried running a rope bridle from the anchor warp to a point near the stern, hoping to change our angle to the swells and produce a more tolerable motion. It seemed to work, allowing us to sleep fitfully.

No one was in any fit state to sail on the next ebb, so we decided to wait for another 12 hours. We might have been there still, but eventually "Dorothy Ann" swung, bringing the anchor warp, held by the bridle, across her stem, where she made short work of sawing it in half. Vicki and I were quickly on deck, realised what had caused the changed motion and started the motor. We spent a little time looking to see if the end of the warp was floating, though we didn't expect it to, finally deciding that if it was, we would more likely get it around the propeller. We must have been recovering a little by then, because we just grinned at each other, hoisted sail without needing to say a word and set off at a tremendous pace down Spithead.

To be sailing again, with a decent beam wind, was just what we needed. It was far too long since any of the adults had been at sea; we needed to get back our confidence and practise our skills. That sail past Southampton Water and up the Solent to Hurst fort was just the tonic we needed.

Darkness was falling once more, as we moved slowly through a curtain of rain, looking unsuccessfully for the lighthouse beam. The wind had at last fallen light again, so we had the Yanmar diesel thudding happily away. We switched on our brand new masthead navigation light. It shone brightly, fine, except that the red port light shone out to starboard, the starboard green to port, both of them facing astern instead of ahead, and the white stern section of the light shining gaily forward. It couldn't have turned around, it was keyed into its socket at the masthead and Bob had put it on the mast cap to stay there. What Bob does can be trusted to stay done. It was a complete mystery and remained so until I was able to get up the mast much later on. Right now, although conditions were much improved, there was going to be no mast climbing. We had an alternative set of lights, for fitting on the shrouds, lower down. We had not had time to fit them before leaving, but now it would be easier to do so than to attempt to cure the problem at the masthead.

Eventually we found the lighthouse, which we had failed to realise was screened from our direction, for its own inscrutable reasons. We anchored safely, using our chain this time, set our riding light and, well clear of the deep water channel, slept peacefully. We awoke to a placid day and motored out over glassy swells into the channel.

We worked our way westward then, with winds

variable in strength and direction. Apart from some alarms in the night, caused by the unpredictable behaviour of French trawlers (or other people's trawlers in French waters, maybe) we had no problems for several days. We were to discover that fishing boats are always a problem at night. They travel very slowly when actually fishing, stop for long periods to haul in their gear, then suddenly set off at high speed for new grounds. Unlike big ships, whose behaviour can be predicted and which can usually be trusted to go safely away once they are past, fishing boats have to be watched constantly and are liable to suddenly reappear over the horizon from some totally unexpected direction.

That would not be too bad if it were all. The real problem is caused by the fact that they invariably have great numbers of enormous deck lights and at least one red light or illuminated curtain on the starboard side. So, whereas it is quite easy to determine the course of a big ship at night by simply looking at its navigation lights, a fishing boat could be pointing anywhere. One clear but moonless night, when the black wave tops glistened in faint starlight and the wind was a powerful but not overwhelming force four to five, I actually overtook a trawler which I was trying to sail away from; simply because, in the galaxy of white and red lights on his starboard side, no green ever became visible at all. We were very close indeed by the time I worked out the cause of our strange tendency to approach each other, on what I had supposed to be diverging courses, and it was with great relief that I made a smart course alteration to pass astern of him.

We could see the loom of the lighthouse at Ushant making its bright glow in the sky, by the time that the next gale warning came. The forecast was for a northerly gale and we were much too close to the north shore of that dangerous, rock strewn coast at the western end of Brittany. Doubting whether we could clear the channel and escape into the Atlantic before the gale came and drove us south to probable destruction, we altered course to the north whilst there was still time to put a safe distance between us and the shore. All day we struggled to make distance, with a light and fitful wind; only to be rewarded, as darkness fell, with a rising wind from the south. This developed into force seven as it blasted us westward past the Scilly Isles, then swung into the southwest and drove us, struggling vainly against it, northward into the Irish Sea.

The weather pattern for that time of year is quite well known and predictable. It consists of a steady string of "lows" or "depressions" travelling north up the coast of Spain, across the gaping mouth of the Bay of Biscay and on past Land's End into the Irish Sea. It is not unusual for winds of hurricane force to be recorded on the Cornish coast and our course now lay directly into the path of these depressions. As we struggled and fought, with reduced sail, for every inch we could get to the southward, we were obliged to go further and further west into the Atlantic. The alternative was to tack into the Bay of Biscay itself, from which we might find it difficult or even impossible to escape. Only once have we ever departed from this sound principle of going well to seaward of any dangerous coastal area!

The B.B.C. marine weather forecasts, listened to with hope of better things in store, became heralds of doom and despair. Force seven we expected, though when it came from ahead we could make little progress against it. Force eight we had experienced, though rarely and in sheltered waters. Force nine we had sailed in only once, with consequences not calculated to increase our confidence. Yet these were indeed forecast, in sequence, duly arrived, dealt with us in their fashion and gave way to the next.

Things broke. Not, as might be expected, at the height of wind and wave; perhaps because we reduced sail in good time to keep the strain on the boat, and more importantly ourselves, within limits. It was when we piled on sail to gain some advantage from the dying winds and the few fair spells between gales that breakages occurred, putting the final strain on flawed equipment weakened by the earlier loads.

First to fail, was the bowsprit, 15 ft long and projecting 10 ft forward of the bow. It snapped with a mighty bang, releasing a flailing mass of wood and chain, flying from the tack of the large Genoa jib which set from the masthead and overlapped the mainsail. We tamed it in the end, lashing the broken pieces to the saloon table for later attention and further restricting our passage through the interior to our bunks. The cause was a faulty bronze shackle which had cracked, characteristically, across the bend. We had all three checked the rigging for these shackles, replacing any which we found with galvanised steel; this one had escaped our notice.

The tiller snapped, predictably, at a point where it had been reduced in thickness to fit a new rudder. The rudder itself had been carefully and expertly built by Andy; unfortunately he had been overloaded with urgent work and had delegated the final fitting to an employee, an excellent woodworker but perhaps less aware of the forces experienced by an ocean going boat. I had seen the weakness myself, but had too many other problems to cope with, so had hoped it would suffice until I could devise a method of strengthening it. I had, however, provided a strong, if inelegant, steel spare, which was quickly fitted in its place. Somehow, in a brief lull, the lower set of navigation lights were fitted to the shrouds and wired up. An entertaining job, with the shrouds slackening and snapping tight as we rolled; trying to work one-handed and hang on with the other.

We were coping quite well. There were problems with the breakages and we were still finding out how to handle "Dorothy Ann" under different conditions, but we were learning as we went along. The food stowage arrangements had worked quite well; the main problem being surpluses of some foods because people had not felt much like eating at the start. One unexpected blow was that Bob was still feeling unwell. We had supposed that after a week or so at sea he would become accustomed to the motion and have no further trouble. We were wrong. Although not always feeling ill, he was almost constantly depressed, especially as each deterioration in the weather caused him further misery.

One thing which was not helping at all was the fact that the deck seam caulking had once more begun to dissolve, allowing water to seep between the planks and saturate our bedding whenever there was sea breaking over the decks, which was often the case. Bob's bunk was subject to some of the worst leaks, which we never in fact managed to eliminate. Also, he found it almost impossible to sleep during the daytime, when the children were at their noisiest, so that his night watches were an agony of tiredness. He became morose and uncommunicative, which was worrying and depressing for the rest of us too. Worst of all he simply could not eat very much, becoming thin and weak as a result. He never missed a watch, was always prompt when his turn was due, but was very, very unhappy.

We struggled onward, the forecasts now working steadily up the Beaufort scale; force eight, nine, ten, eleven. "ELEVEN ?" No. We didn't want to believe it. But it came anyway, tearing the sea apart with winds which drove water droplets like pebbles before them. Looking out into the wind was impossible; looking anywhere was pointless, since the air was an opaque mass of atomised water and salt. Even breathing was difficult in the wet, salty atmosphere. Then the wind dropped abruptly, releasing the seas from its grip, to rear, without reason or pattern, in monstrous pyramids which fell upon us, crashing green through the small gap where one washboard was left out from the hatchway, to provide minimal ventilation.

In those days, when we always steered by hand, the poor helmsman was regularly submerged in a curtain of green water in bad conditions, and we learned to sit stoically holding our breath until it drained away. Those below would look out anxiously to see if the helmsman was still there, but nobody was ever washed out of the cockpit. We were always attached to the boat by our safety harnesses, even so, it would have been uncomfortable and dangerous to be dragged along overside. That storm, we were later told by a friend connected with the

N.A.S.A. weather reporting organisation, had begun as a West Indies hurricane, crossed the Atlantic, and become rejuvenated as it joined the chain of North Atlantic lows. It achieved some notoriety by sinking several yachts and a ship, with some loss of life; facts of which we remained mercifully ignorant until we reached port. It was the first day of November 1982; the end of our second week at sea.

The mizen boom broke as we were at last making progress to the south, on the final ragged tails of the storm. A weak spot right in its centre allowed it to collapse gently into a dog leg shape, held together by several layers of sail, as we were reefed at the time and the mizen had roller reefing; which wound the lower part of the sail into a rather untidy roll around the boom, but was easy to use. The whole lot, an unwieldy 14ft mass of wood and cloth, was unbolted at the gooseneck, unlaced from the mast, and taken below to join the ever growing pile tied to the table. It was, however, the last failure on that leg.

Sails had, as they always do, chafed away their stitching in innumerable places. Both large headsails required extensive re-sewing; also the hanks which hold the luff of the sail to the forestay had pulled out completely, in a very short space of time. These were new sails which we had bought especially for the trip. The 20 year old sails which came with the boat gave no trouble for many more miles. So when the wind finally fell light, as we passed the latitude of Cape Finisterre and edged our way cautiously along the coastal shipping lane, the cockpit was filled with an all engulfing mass of sailcloth, as we sewed frantically in order to be able to make any progress at all.

Our original plan had been to make our first stop at Gibraltar; Vicki and I are probably sufficiently stubborn to have tried to stick to that, despite the gear failures which had occurred. Bob, though, finally had to admit defeat and asked to be put ashore as soon as possible. I doubted if we would get out of any of the Biscay ports, once in, so opted for Vigo, which is reached from the west coast of Spain. It was a wise and necessary decision for us also, I now believe, giving us a much needed chance to rest and recuperate.

Through swirling mists we caught a brief glimpse of land, high peaks or islands, it was difficult to judge. Thumbing through the illustrations in the Admiralty Pilot for that coast, I was able to identify the outline as Islas Cies, the islands lying in the mouth of the "ria" or inlet, which leads to the port of Vigo. I have never since made a certain identification of a landfall in that way, often being entirely unable to relate anything in sight to either written or pictorial illustration. This once we were lucky. The fog closed in almost at once, but we had the compass bearing by then and were able to proceed with confidence. The Spanish lights are sensibly placed high up on the rocks and so are visible for some distance even in bad visibility, because the mist tends to be much thinner overhead than all around. As darkness fell, the welcome sight of the light on Islas Cies was seen and identified.

The wind had fallen away completely as we entered the ria. The Atlantic swells arrive upon that coast after their unimpeded journey of several thousands of miles, driving violently onward into the inlet. As we motored in, it became an acrobatic feat to lower and stow the sails on the wildly rolling deck. Then the rain came. It was good inasmuch as it dispersed the fog completely, allowing us to see the lighted buoys ahead. Motoring in rain though, must be about my least favourite pastime. Standing still at the tiller, motor running steadily and deafeningly, water inexorably creeping inside the neck of my oilskin coat, chilled hands in saturated gloves; I really can't recommend it.

Vicki peered through the hatchway, giving a steady stream of directions: "Turn 85 degrees to port, head for the red light occulting every three seconds, after half a mile you should see two white lights to starboard, turn to starboard when they are in line..." and so on. Juggling with chart and lights list, with never a look outside, she directed us faultlessly up the twisting channel for hours until, at last, we could see the mooring buoys at the Real Club Nautico de Vigo. The rain stopped then and with the help of people from another boat we got a line ashore, lying stern toward the quay with our bow line to the buoy.

I didn't relish the thought of cooking after that, although I was certainly hungry enough. I had become ship's cook by default, when Vicki's unexpected sickness made her quite unable to work in the galley. It was a good arrangement normally; I was quite happy to cook and fortunately quite competent also. There was only a problem when, as in the preceding several hours, there were conflicting demands on my time. Now I was just too tired to bother. I was about to receive the first of quite a number of pleasant surprises, provided by the family which I had, despite my confidence in them, seriously underestimated.

In short, Catherine, then aged 11, had cooked supper. I went below and discovered plates of steaming Spaghetti Bolognaise ready on the table, with a bottle of wine appropriate to a celebration meal. Bob climbed sheepishly out of his bunk and the six of us sat down to the first real enjoyment together since leaving Littlehampton 26 days before. Only when we were sated, warm and happy, did Catherine tell us how near we had come to going hungry that night. A violent roll of the boat at a critical moment had thrown the spaghetti clear out of the saucepan but she, with commendable aplomb, had picked it up and thrown it right back in again.

Bob had really taken considerable physical punishment. His clothing hung loosely upon him as though intended for someone two sizes larger and his walk was that of an elderly or infirm person. The combination of seasickness and the difficulty of an essentially solitary person trying to adapt to life in exceptionally close proximity to a noisy, argumentative, active family, was too great a strain. He could not go on, yet with so much committed and so many high hopes of adventure, how could he take the decision to quit? And there is the worst task that a skipper must face; taking a decision which must do harm to someone, for the overall good of ship and crew. Hard enough if it were a casually met crew member. So much harder to persuade a dear friend who has thrown heart and soul into the venture, suffering discomfort, inconvenience and financial loss, to abandon all hope of receiving the eventual rewards which are no less than his due. I know I had no choice but to push Bob into the decision to give up, but I shall always wish there had been another way.

Decision made however, Bob became at least a semblance of his old competent self. Briskly arranging his flight home, he set off intending to return by road with a vehicle suitable for collecting his possessions from on board. His description of the flight to the U.K. is a small gem and a measure of our loss in not having his talents available to describe our later adventures; one of which was the direct outcome of his leaving.

The telegram arrived a week later, when we were in the throes of trying to repair the various broken items of gear. "Regret unable to return. Expect carrier imminently," it said, enigmatically. What did it mean? Would "carrier" be a well organised international company, versed in customs procedures and armed with crates, boxes and packing materials? Was imminently tomorrow, in a few days, next week, soon? Bob had on board the normal accoutrements of the Englishman contemplating a lengthy sojourn in foreign parts; umbrella, fishing rod, cameras, fins, snorkel, wetsuit, communications receiver, barograph. . . . Of course a number of things were his contribution to the overall total for common use and generously he had told us to retain on board whatever was of use to us. However, we feared that some things, such as the barograph and the radio, were too liable to damage from the effects of salt water and would just be pointlessly ruined if not returned now.

We decided to pack the items as best we could, to at least protect them when ferrying them ashore in the dinghy. It was as well that we did. We crammed things into bags and cases, tied up the radio in a sleeping bag, filled two large sacks with other items and just completed the task as a small Spanish removal van drove onto the quay. The driver and his mate, neither of whom spoke English, managed to tell us somehow that they were indeed "carrier", as expected, and we began the task of ferrying dinghy loads of packages ashore.

We were hardly assisted by the seven foot swell running in the bay at that time. Each time the dinghy approached the stone steps set in the side of the harbour wall, the removal men would start down to meet us. Then the swell would run in, climbing rapidly, seven feet up the steps as the men rushed hastily back upward and I, borne up almost to the top hurled packages across before dropping sickeningly down, as a mass of water poured down off the open side of the steps into the dinghy. At the boat end of the operation the swell, rebounding from the wall, met the next incoming one, creating a short, steep sea which caused boat and dinghy to rise and fall wildly out of phase with one another, so that passing packages across became a sort of athletic feat. It took about eight trips in all, for there were 56 packages, by which time we were glad to stand on dry land for a while.

We had just closed the door on the last package when a uniformed, gun draped figure came running along the quay. He plainly wished us to cease and desist from our activities, so we stood and awaited his coming. "Aha" I thought, "a Customs officer. Now the International Carriers will produce correct documentation and all will be well." No, you're right; they didn't. There was confused milling until a passer by who spoke perfect English volunteered to assist. Basil did his best for us, but officialdom decreed that we should proceed to customs headquarters, at the nearby International terminal. Vicki and I joined the driver and his mate in the front of the van, an armed guard was placed in the back and off we went. Vicki and I knew we weren't going far, but for the children, alone for the first time in a foreign country and marooned on the boat, since the dinghy was now ashore, it was a horrific experience, watching us disappear.

Explanations were given, higher officials were called, explanations repeated, phone calls to mysterious destinations made, more explanations requested. No one was unpleasant or even impolite, the regulations had clearly been infringed in some way and no one was quite sure what should be done. Eventually all the packages were unloaded and counted. Eleven people counted and got six different totals. It took about an hour for everyone to agree. We were then asked to get a Customs Agent to sort matters out, which we did with the help of the British Consul. The goods finally reached England three months later, mostly none the worse for their treatment and still packed as we had left them. In addition to a hefty bill for the carriage Bob was required to pay £50 as part share of a fine, for what, he was never told! It was over a year later, when we were very practised in entering strange ports, that I realised that none of the officials for whom I had filled in forms or signed things, on arrival in Vigo, had been in Customs uniform. So I think the whole problem was caused by failing to clear in properly in the first place.

The tiller was repaired and strengthened. The bowsprit also, though somewhat shorter than before. The mizen boom was shortened as well, making it impossible to set the original sail. We managed however to set the old mainsail from our previous boat as a mizen. It was a bit small, but it served well and we were glad we had kept it when the new one was fitted, and not sold it with "Geisha".

We had also to investigate the mystery of the navigation lights. Though the lower set had been fitted at sea, giving us at least some means of showing our presence, the masthead light was more easily visible and drew less current from our limited electrical supply. I hauled myself up in a "bosun's chair", rolling and banging against the mast and shrouds, to the very top. The answer to the riddle of the reversed lights was very simple. The coloured glass screen inside the lamp was "secured" by a tiny dab of glue, which had soon let go when subjected to the accelerations normally present at a masthead in rough weather. A modification, the first of many on that lamp, secured it immovably from then onward.

Repairs finished at last, we prepared to leave. We got to bed early, arose refreshed and prepared for a perfectly planned departure. Then the gear lever connecting rod bent in half, due to rust stiffening the action at the gearbox end, so I spent eight hours fixing it and we left at 4 p.m. dog tired and in falling darkness. Why not wait till next day? Well, sometimes we fear that one delay will lead to another until the voyage grinds to a halt altogether. Besides we had to see if we could manage without Bob, and the sooner we left the sooner we would know the answer.

Diana wrote a poem:

Sailing on the sea, sailing on the sea,
The waves go "splish", the waves go "splosh",
Wind in the rigging, water on me,
That is the price you have to pay,
When you're sailing on the sea.

7
Settling Down

Finally we set off down the ria. As soon as we were clear of the mooring, and of the ferries which criss cross the bay from the little dock alongside the Real Club Nautico, we prepared to hoist sail. The wind was fair and moderate; we should be able to motor gently onward with the helm automatically controlled (I won't name the wretched device, but there is a clue there for the knowledgeable) whilst we both handled the sails. The automatic helm control had been tried out briefly in the few quieter periods on the way down and had seemed barely adequate, although allegedly suitable for 35 ft yachts. Still, it had worked and under these quiet conditions it should be capable of holding a compass course for a few minutes. No way. It had, in the interim, died altogether, never to work again. At about £350 for four hours' work it hardly struck us as a good use of our limited funds for the journey. It wasn't quite called an Autolemon, but it might as well have been.

We got the sails up anyway, with much dashing back to the helm to keep us out in the middle of the channel; it is quite wide, but there are rocks here and there, toward which any self respecting boat will head unerringly if allowed to do so. Once we were settled down, with the working sails set, we went into our night watchkeeping routine of three hours on watch, three hours off, repeated once more to cover a 12 hour period. This was followed by three, four hour, day watches, so that we would each do one four hour watch on one day and two on the next. We reasoned that three hours on the helm was the most we could manage at night, but anything less than three hours was inadequate for the off watch person to sleep. Day watches are less of a strain and so could be a little longer. The odd number of watches resulted in a different pattern each day, which helped to avoid monotony. Although changed to cope with emergencies, this pattern served us well for three years, after which the children began to take a regular part in the watchkeeping routine. At no time did we sail without keeping a watch.

Our ability was soon put to the test. The wind strength rose steadily as darkness fell, so that soon it became a struggle to stay on course. It was a fair wind at last, so we were running with our great gaff sails boomed well out, pulling hard to one side and requiring all our strength to remain on course. Despite using tiller lines to take some of the strain (the tiller was deeply grooved with the evidence of their past use) Vicki was exhausted after only two hours. I soon discovered that I too was unlikely to manage for the whole of my watch, so I began to experiment to see how some of the enormous tension on the main sheet could be used as power assistance for the tiller. I was not then trying to achieve full self steering, although I had read what books I could find on the subject, with the intention of later attempting to devise such a system. However, when I had linked sheet to tiller via a rather "Heath Robinson" system of ropes and pulleys, I found to my surprise that not only was my arm no longer pulled out of its socket, I could go below and make a cup of tea whilst we still roared happily along on our course.

That system, with a number of modifications to enable it to cope with different wind strengths and directions, was in use for the rest of the voyage. We never again hand steered except in the proximity of land or shipping, or when motoring in calms. It was effective when under both sail and power, provided there was a reasonable wind strength. The effectiveness varied with wind and sea conditions, but it became unusual to have to go out into the cockpit unless there was a wind shift, or a course change was needed. It became normal practice just to stand up in the hatchway every ten minutes to look round, then go below again and get on with something else. There was a useful lesson in this. Keep it simple.

Things made of rope and wood may wear out and go wrong, but they are very easy and relatively cheap to repair or replace. The cautious use of advanced technology is an excellent thing; modern synthetic ropes and sailcloth are a joy to use, as are waterproof resin glues. It is by using these advances carefully, in conjunction with traditional ways, developed also through many years of trial and error under harsh conditions, that reliability is achieved. And at sea reliability is everything. Failure can be fatal.

On Christmas Day the galley stove collapsed. Well, the stove itself, bought secondhand at Beaulieu Boat Jumble, for £15, was fine, but the swinging frame which allowed it to remain level as the boat heeled had worn out. That had cost £35, brand new and supplied by the stove manufacturers. Another of my pet hates is the way companies can be bought up and their standards of workmanship allowed to deteriorate, yet the original name is preserved to delude the customer. One finds time to ponder such questions at sea and it is difficult to keep politics out of a book of this kind. Perhaps what really rankles is the fact that the year after we bought the frame I saw a whole box of those going cheaply at Beaulieu too! As a special treat for me, Vicki had volunteered to cook Christmas dinner. So she did, but having spent my entire watch below rebuilding the cooker frame instead of sleeping, I was in no state to really appreciate it. Also, because I had been repairing the frame throughout the whole of her watch on deck, she could not start cooking until she, also, should have been sleeping. Fortunately the weather had moderated and we were enjoying fair winds, with sunshine even, as we opened our presents in the cockpit, off the Portugese coast, some way west of Lisbon.

We had tried to phone relatives in England, via V.H.F. radio and the Coast radio station, but had been unable to do so. We had, however, raised a large number of drunken but gallant Portugese fishermen who, inspired by the sound of Vicki's voice on the radio, attempted to simulate the shore station and carry on a suggestive conversation. We didn't begrudge them their amusement, though it was disappointing to realise that we had not managed to raise the Coast radio station after all. We were to hear much stranger things on V.H.F. later in the voyage.

The run to Vila Moura, on the south coast of Portugal, was pleasant and uneventful. We spent three days at the large marina there, celebrating Catherine's 11th birthday on December 28th. Then on to Gibraltar, keeping as well clear of the solid line of shipping in the straits as we could; thankful for light winds which allowed us to motor sail well inshore of them. We crept nervously, in the dark, between the shadowy shapes of huge tankers moored in the bay, were alarmed by the sudden sight of the airport runway in the water right ahead of us, edged cautiously past the Morocco ferry and slid with relief alongside the arrivals dock.

The Gibraltarian officials cleared us in with little fuss, directing us to the reception dock of the new marina. Next morning we were allocated a berth inside, to which we moved "Dorothy Ann"; afterwards setting out to explore the town. It was, of course, a Sunday; followed, inevitably, by a public holiday. On such days there are no banks open and the traveller naturally has no money. Luckily for us Gibraltar boasts that wonderfully useful institution, the money changer. These people, not being part of any large, indifferent company or, worse, government department, feel obliged to offer a service to their customers when it is actually needed. One hopes that they become deservedly rich as a result, particularly as their rates are modest. One of the virtues of travelling by boat is that, provided the provisioning is carefully planned and carried out, it is possible to go on eating and sleeping without immediate access to local currency. But it is unquestionably more fun to walk up Main Street with at least some cash in one's pocket. Fresh milk and bread which someone else has had to bake are great luxuries.

Vicki, writing home on January 3rd said ". . . Just think, we haven't had a bath since 16th Oct! (Only showers)." Also "Lessons are going very well. The girls do three to four hours a day, except Sundays, and seem to enjoy doing it. The only problem is that it takes me ages to prepare and mark the lessons..." And "...We've walked around Gib. looking for a telephone box (a British one it says in all the glossy brochures; it doesn't add that, like the British ones, they are all out of order)." She also talked about the watch system working well, adding "The only time we break the 'Rule' is if there is an emergency or we are coming into port, when we can catch up on our sleep later."

One of Vicki's earliest priorities was to find a sailmaker. She wanted to reduce the size of the mizen, so that we could have a shorter, more manageable boom. Although quite competent at sail and rope work, she felt that this was too major a task to tackle on her own. I thought she was right, not through any lack of expertise, but because that expensive white elephant of a sewing machine would have been hard put to mend a pair of pyjamas without breaking down at least three times. The job was done expertly and quite inexpensively, turning the mizen from a nightmare into the most tractable and useful sail we have ever owned.

On the end of the quay leading to the marina there is a Lipton's supermarket. It seems very proper for a sailor to buy his provisions from the company once owned by the famous Sir Thomas, each of whose yachts cost more than most of us will see in a lifetime. A more basic reason to shop there is the large variety of English canned goods, particularly meat, to be found there. In Spain we had found our choice limited to a very few varieties of most oddly flavoured products; a problem which we had quite failed to anticipate.

We had plenty of stores for our current use, but now we were anxious to ensure an adequate supply of our favourites as far as Australia, if possible. One thing we had learned is that joyfully experimenting with unusual meals ashore is one thing, being stuck miles out at sea with only things which you dislike to eat is purgatory. We filled two supermarket carts to capacity and somehow stowed the contents aboard. At least we were able to load from the quay directly across onto the stern of the boat; much better than having to haul everything in the dinghy. Due to the regular dispute between Britain and Spain over the Sovereignty of Gibraltar, no fresh vegetables were being imported from Spain at that time, and those flown in from Morocco were expensive and of poor quality. Accordingly we planned to visit the Spanish port of Estapona, where fresh food was available in abundance.

Meanwhile, we indulged in a little tourism. We discovered the London Pub, which had all the attributes of an English pub, plus staying open all day and having no restriction on the children accompanying us. We climbed the rock, photographed the apes, explored the tunnels and rode in the cable cars.

Just as we were ready to leave I found the list of agents for the repair of the awful automatic helming device (or Autolemon) which I had mislaid, and discovered that the neighbouring yard, the famous Shepherds, was the local agent. I therefore called upon them and, after waiting in a cold and empty chandlery for about half an hour, I was rewarded with a few moments of an assistant's time. It was, I learned, quite impossible that anyone in the wintry desertion of the business could spare the time to perform a quick check on the unit; perhaps assessing the likelihood of repair being possible. There were forms to be filled in, a proper and dignified waiting period to be observed; also, I began to feel, perhaps a Papal dispensation to be obtained before it could be admitted to the chosen few. There is only one sensible reaction to that sort of "service". I left, taking my useless electronic device with me, and sailed for Estapona.

The journey to Estapona was pleasant; an uneventful one day sail in light winds, which resulted in another night arrival, our third in four ports. There was mild confusion as the night watchman indicated an empty berth and could not understand our subsequent manoeuvres as "Dorothy Ann" declined to answer her rudder when put astern, forcing us to adopt a shuffling, crabwise approach. Finally alongside, I busied myself adjusting ropes, looking around eventually to find Vicki and a group of Spanish Customs officers teaching each other numbers in their respective languages – in the middle of the night.

We stayed only one day, despite being made to feel wonderfully welcome, for we wanted to reach Australia without undue delay. The local market was fairly bursting with vegetables of top quality, of which we bought an enormous load. On the way back to the marina we stopped to buy bread. As it was now late on Friday evening and the baker wished to clear his stock, he filled a huge sack with bread for the price of two loaves. Finally we discovered that, whereas we had paid to top up our tanks with brackish water in Gibraltar, the water in Estapona was fresh, clear and free. Hastily we drained and refilled the tanks.

We set off for our next port, Cagliari, on the Italian island of Sardinia, in calm weather. It was a curiously mild and windless day, prompting us to set both topsails for the first time. The surface of the sea was dotted with dolphins and killer whales, just lying basking in the sun, a sight we have never again seen anywhere in the world. The entire day had a breathless magical quality, so still and silent that we spoke in whispers and moved about the decks on tiptoe.

At dusk the spell was shattered. Just as the light on Cabo de Gata, the easternmost corner of Spain, began to swing its beam across the sea; just as the usual stream of lighted shipping converged on the point, where we were virtually becalmed, we were knocked flat by a sudden vicious gust of wind. Vicki, on watch, scrambled forward on the sloping deck and succeeded somehow in getting the large foresail off and lashing it to the pulpit. Then, half exhausted, she called me to help. In view of the obvious urgency I wasted as little time as possible on getting ready, but I really cannot recommend underpants, an oilskin jacket and a safety harness, as sole evening wear on a winter's night in the Mediterranean. Still, as I was regularly immersed for the next few hours, it did reduce the number of garments to be saturated.

By the time I reached the foredeck, the sea had snatched at the foresail, dragging it over the side and cracking the stainless steel pulpit. I got it back by dragging its sopping mass into my lap, a method which was to become all too familiar in the times to come. Once that was bagged and stowed, oozing, below, I freed the main topsail, since I could do nothing to reduce the mainsail whilst it was set. Once free, it flew like a kite until it stalled, dropping its 20ft long yard to the deck endways on, within inches of my feet.

After that it was just hard work. It took five hours altogether, for us to get the working sails off and the storm sails set. The children, with a degree of initiative and skill which we had never imagined, had prepared tea, soup and sandwiches. There were no more doubts; we were a crew and together we could take anything which came. Vicki and I resorted to an old trick which we had used when driving long distances; one of us slept for half an hour, then the other for an hour, then the first for two hours, then we were able to resume normal watches.

That storm, coming from nowhere in less than half an hour, lasted for three days. Once again it was "on the nose" and we tacked so close to the North African coast that we could identify the lights of Oran. I experienced some queasiness at first, but an 11 hour spell lying face down in the bilges coaxing a recalcitrant diesel engine to start, so that we could recharge the batteries for the navigation lights, left me numbed to all feeling.

We tacked back toward Spain, down again toward Africa; after three days, when the weather began to moderate, we had sailed 180 miles through the water. We were 20 miles closer to our destination.

One more equally abrupt and savage gale struck us as we were within a day's sail of Cagliari. This time a snarl up of ropes on the foredeck led to me sitting helplessly unravelling a vast ball of matted lines whilst £1,000 worth of foresails thrashed themselves to pieces above my head and flailing sheets battered me almost senseless.

We sighted Cagliari from afar, the gale having passed on with merciful speed overnight. Excited by the apparent nearness, despite the evidence of the chart, we abandoned the watch system and spent long hours on deck together. As a result, we were both very tired by the time when we finally approached the port. At the first cluster of masts which we approached we were waved vigorously away, subsequent wavings more encouragingly indicating the direction to go in.

Threading our way nervously past sleek Italian ferries, sidling across the bows of moored but pulsating tugs, we eventually made our way into the little dock where the transit moorings are. It began to rain steadily.

Our first week was miserable. We could speak no Italian and, except for the busy Port Captain, no one could speak English. It was cold, it rained and it blew. We had some laundry done, with memories of Spanish and Portugese prices. The bill was horrific, and we were reduced to washing the remainder on board. This extra duty consumed our stocks of paraffin rapidly, and also caused the stove burners to clog. We had spare burners, so we were able to change them and clean the old ones at our leisure. Eventually though, the old burners failed for various reasons, and we arranged to have new replacements sent. They were not tried out until we were at sea, when it was discovered that there were tiny pinholes in them, rendering them useless. We were always able to keep one burner in service, becoming adept at producing one burner meals. Had that failed, we had a single burner Primus in reserve, of an antiquated and hence virtually indestructible design.

We also used paraffin lamps; wick lamps for general use, a "Tilley" pressure lamp for brilliant light. The Tilley was also our cabin heater in those clammy days and very effective it was too, a feature which was less welcome in the tropics. Eventually it needed a new burner tube. We really ought not to have been surprised when the replacement buckled and became useless after one evening's use. No doubt it had been "value engineered", a salesman's euphemism for being made shoddy and useless.

We always found stocks of paraffin eventually, once we discovered what to ask for locally. In Cagliari we tried "Petrolio", as given in our dictionary, but to no avail. Total incomprehension resulted. The magic word, it transpired, was "Kerosina" which, when finally tracked down, came in a large can inscribed with a statement that it was "Petrolio", suitably treated for use in domestic heating systems!

When the rain stopped, we dragged out the shredded foresails and tried to assemble the various pieces on the quay, in a sort of large, cloth jigsaw. We also carried forth the wretched sewing machine, more in hope than anger, after the usual three hour de-rusting session. Whilst Vicki was weighting down various pieces of cloth and the wind was blowing them free again, two Italian girls came down the quay with their large German Shepherd dog. The dog made a beeline for the sewing machine and, before I could shout a warning, thoroughly baptised the thing. The girls fled in embarrassment, dragging the puzzled dog with them. I could not help thinking, as I hosed the machine down, that the dog probably had the right idea. I only wish it had been the manufacturer rather than the product.

The masthead light was once again giving problems. One bulb had failed and the other was so idiotically mounted that it broke as I tried to remove it. No joke, when the replacements, sent from England as they were not stocked locally, cost £10 each. I later discovered that they are a third of that price in the U.S.A. More glue gave way and I drilled and tapped in screws to hold it together with some hope of remaining in one piece. I won't give its real name but, since it appeared to have been designed by a sheep with a particularly small brain, I shall call it Merinospeck.

Of course it was not all, or even mostly, gloom and doom. After the first ghastly week we made friends; a few hardy yachtsmen, some R.A.F. personnel (my old service) from the local N.A.T.O. base. The butcher and greengrocer were working hard at our Italian, the butcher refusing to give me my meat until I repeated the name of the cut correctly, the greengrocer engaging Vicki in animated and remarkably comprehensible conversation. Even the old chap who swept the quay and fed the pigeons used to stop and chat.

Our friend Eric departed on the bus, wearing the broken pulpit around his neck and shoulders and causing chaos in the, fortunately wide, doorway. He returned it neatly welded, also bringing a large baulk of timber which later became a new mizen boom. We crammed of an evening into our saloon for pancake parties and enjoyed hilarious feasts, with a crowd of many nationalities, aboard a neighbouring boat.

A great discovery was the "Vende Vini", a wine cooperative which sold its produce from pumps identical to those at petrol filling stations. The minimum quantity sold was five litres, but at those prices we did not limit ourselves to the minimum. Certain of our friends had discovered even cheaper wine, which they termed "Vino Collapso", with good cause. So with work, goodwill and help from our friends, an unbeatable recipe for success, our problems were overcome. A last day of relaxed hilarity, when yet another gale pinned us in the harbour, and we departed for Greece.

Earlier plans to visit Malta had been shelved when we learned that we would be charged for a minimum of three weeks' mooring. The cost was not unreasonable for a three week stay, but for our proposed visit of three days it was ludicrously expensive. Our letters enquiring if this was indeed the case had been unanswered, by both the Tourist Ministry and the Yacht Club, so we opted for the direct route to Greece, north of Sicily and through the Straits of Messina.

Many ocean going sailors must have experienced the feeling of disbelieving horror as the red glow of a big ship's port navigation light looms above them, terrifyingly close, where a moment ago the ocean was completely empty. Sometimes, I suppose, they may really have been inattentive; the ship really is there and probably they perish. It is far more likely though that, provided they do not expire instantly from cardiac arrest, they subsequently find that it is just the moon rising, behind a bank of haze. We had by now seen enough moon risings to be aware of this phenomenon, so when a red glow appeared in the sky ahead of us I was not alarmed. I knew, I thought, that it must be the moon. Then it flamed and spread across the base of the clouds, causing my hair to stand on end and my skin to come out in goose pimples. Somewhere ahead, in the night, Stromboli was advertising its presence. I soon realised the cause, but my heart rate took a long time to return to normal.

The Straits of Messina, home of the legendary whirlpools Scylla and Charybdis, demand a cautious approach. Though changes in the bottom contours have lessened the dangers which beset the heroes of ancient Greece, a far greater hazard to the small boat sailor is posed by the many ferries which ply across this narrow strip of water. These vessels have, and demand, absolute right of way, and are reputed to have rammed small boats which have impeded them. A natural hazard which remains is the tidal bore, a moving wall of water several feet high caused by the passage of a large body of water from the Ionian to the Tyrrhenian sea, through the narrow neck of the straits, at each turn of the tide. We timed our approach carefully. It was the evening of the day following the sighting of Stromboli.

We had spent the early hours huddled together in the cockpit; eating chocolate and watching the volcano as it gave a spectacular juggling display, throwing red hot rocks into the air in a stream of molten lava, followed after a breathless pause by a deep rumbling roar, which made the boat, and us, tremble. At dawn we had rounded Strombolicci, an isolated pinnacle which guards the approach to the straits. All day we had sailed quietly under a grey but non threatening sky. Now we sailed, in quiet conditions, to and fro along the northern coast of Sicily, as we waited for the bore to pass through the straits. We read and re-read the Admiralty Pilot, checked the tide tables and our watches again, but always concluded that it was not safe to enter the straits until just after nightfall.

At last it was 10.30 p.m. We turned and headed for the narrow "dog leg" opening to the straits. A patrolling Pilot Cutter swung his spotlight to direct us to the safest path and we slipped between the sites of the ancient whirlpools to approach the modern danger of the ferries.

By judicious adjustment of our speed, using both sail and power, once we had studied the paths and timings of the various ferry services, we slipped safely through into the darkness of the lower straits. Suddenly, as we relaxed from running the gauntlet of the ferry tracks, we were laid on our side again. The katabatic winds, formed by an enormous volume of cold air abruptly sliding down the mountain slopes, had struck us.

Identifying a meteorological phenomenon is one thing. Dealing with it is quite another, I reflected as I struggled once more to reduce sail. I suppose I ought to make it clear that although "Dorothy Ann" was often wet, frequently stubborn and sometimes tiring, she was never, ever, frightening. She would duck and weave through the most monstrous seas, rolling wildly and sometimes slamming down like a falling lift, but she took hardly any water aboard, and showed not the slightest tendency to roll dangerously far, dig her bows in, or allow water over her stern.

Sail was fairly soon reduced sufficiently; we were not carrying too much when the wind rose, so it was a simple matter to drop the mainsail and change to a smaller foresail. We blew down to the southern end of the straits by dawn, whereupon the wind died altogether, leaving us crashing and banging in the heavy seas left by the storm. We could see, just under the mizen boom, Mt Etna smoking steadily in the distance. Two days later it was still there, but eventually a breeze came, to carry us on our way. The Ionian sea presented us with a storm of its own, in which we were obliged to stand off, clear of the rock bound coast of Greece, for two days. Our confidence was badly shaken by a persistent leak which we could not trace and which we feared might suddenly worsen. It transpired to be a broken stern tube, which had allowed the gland around the propeller shaft to leak.

Eventually we docked, and the customary hunt for food, fuel and repairs began. When one is fortunate enough to be moored in the centre of town, or even on its fringes, food shopping is simple enough. Fuel, the ubiquitous kerosene, was easily available too but, as supplied in three square 17 litre cans, a little awkward to carry.

Taxis, we found to our delight, were cheap. Vicki, then, would buy the kerosene, the shop would phone for a taxi and all would be well; as it would have been, but for the belated discovery that the usual swarming mass of taxis had seemingly vanished from the face of the earth. The drivers, so the shopkeeper explained, had chosen this day on which to strike. Refusing to admit defeat, Vicki waited for the bus. The conductor looked dubiously at her three metal cans, but offered no objection, which is one reason why she, rather than I, is sent for these things. When the cap of one can began to leak though, with the lurching of the vehicle, even she began to doubt her powers of persuasion, struggling to keep it hidden from view and pretending not to be aware of the ever increasing reek of fuel.

Thankfully the journey was short and she arrived triumphantly back aboard "Dorothy Ann" to demand the praise which was her due. I bought diesel at the English speaking chandler's across the street, not qualifying for hero treatment.

We were unable to arrange a haul out in Kalamata, our port of arrival, despite a month of yes, no, maybe, tomorrow, type negotiations. Discovering that the problem could easily be cured temporarily with two simple wooden wedges against the adjacent frames, we departed for the island of Rhodos, furthest East of the Greek islands. In Rhodos we were lifted out very cheaply and efficiently on a "Travel Hoist", a machine comprising a huge open framework on wheels, with webbing slings to pass under the boat, which are then raised so that the boat can be lifted out of the water and driven away into the yard. They are common throughout the world now, but we had never seen one in action before and were most impressed.

Once again we shopped in Greek, of which we speak no more than eleven words; the numbers one to ten and "Thank you". This was Vicki's master plan for coping with a wide variety of languages in a short space of time. Learn the numbers and "Thank you" and you can at least indicate willingness to try. Most people respond delightedly, sometimes crediting you with unwonted fluency and replying with a flood of unintelligible phrases.

Our particular friend in Rhodos was the lady who ran the local grocery shop. Without a word of English, but with great interest and determination, she engaged Vicki in conversation. By gestures, photographs and apparently telepathy, they conversed happily for hours. When we forgot our cash and made to set our purchases aside whilst we returned to collect the housekeeping purse, the bill, probably equal to a week's profits, was casually put away for another day and a taxi summoned to carry our goods to the quay. Such trust, on barely a week's acquaintance, is heartwarming indeed.

We were joined in Rhodos by Darwin, a six foot five inch tall American, who somehow coiled his great length into "Dorothy Ann"s spare bunk. He had strolled into the yard seeking work to replenish his funds as he backpacked around the world. We had work aplenty, but could not afford to pay to have it done by others. We offered him a ride as far as he wished, in the general direction of Australia and he accepted. With his vigorous help our work of cleaning off the hull, replacing the stern tube, painting, oiling and minor repairs, was soon completed.

The tiny harbour of Mandraki, its entrance once spanned by the Colossus of Rhodes, one of the original Seven Wonders of the World, was crowded when we first arrived. When we were ready to leave the yard it was packed, the season for chartering having now begun, so we decided to sail straight across to Marmaris, in

Turkey, only a one day sail away.

It was another night arrival but, after an easy day in which Darwin had done much of the work and all of the cooking, "Dorothy Ann", cleaned, painted and with all her gear in good order, consented to manoeuvre with deceptive ease to a berth at the Marmaris quay.

We spent ten days in Turkey and all were pleasant. We gorged ourselves on bread so good that we ate it whole, like huge rolls, also on fresh, juicy olives (a new taste for me, I had never liked them before) and great blocks of white Feta cheese. Our friends from Mandraki, Marty, Hank and Jacqui, of "Salty Dawg" and Colin and Glenys of "Vorastri", were also there. Soon, as always in the yachting world, we made more friends.

We found that, provided we walked one street back, behind the tourist cafes on the waterfront, it was possible to eat enormous, tasty meals, washed down freely with wine, for about £1 per person. That, together with our combined stocks of Ouzo (we had been opposite the wholesalers in Rhodos) made our stay memorable, but hazily so.

A local boatbuilder made us a new bowsprit for £15. Darwin, with his phenomenal energy, planed the baulk of timber from Cagliari to a round section, enabling me to turn it into a boom for our re-cut mizen. We left for Port Said with everything in good shape once more.

8
Eastern Adventures

With Darwin taking watches and insisting on doing the cooking we had an easy, lazy trip to Egypt. Poor Darwin; I had warned him about the red moonrise, but left him alone on watch with instructions to call me if he saw anything at all which bothered him. Sure enough, he called me out of my bunk to investigate a strange red light. By the time we got back on deck of course, the moon had risen a little higher and there was no doubt of what it was. I didn't mind, indeed I was glad to know that my instructions were being carefully followed, but Darwin was kicking himself for not remembering my warning.

We saw an increasing number of ships as we neared the canal. Generally they could be trusted to observe the rule of the road, but a couple of close shaves taught us to avoid getting into a position where our lives would depend on it. A big ship's officer of the watch may know he is going to pass clear by a few feet, but by the time it is certain that he is not it can be too late for the yacht to take avoiding action.

A brisk breeze drove us rapidly through the anchorage area where the big ships assemble for the canal transit. Soon it became a "fresh" breeze, as much as our sails could handle but not yet too much. With an adequate, well rested crew for once, I was happy to hang on to everything, including both topsails and our two largest headsails. That pleased Vicki, who always wants too much sail up anyway.

Suddenly, as our attention was taken up with avoiding two large sunken wrecks, half awash in the approach channel, we found ourselves in the canal. Taken by surprise, but not yet worried, I moved to release the headsails, calling to Vicki to take the tiller. For some reason the halliards of both foresails were jammed, I think probably pulled down tightly on their cleats by the high strain on them. Rushing aft to drop the mizen topsail, I found that the boom, hard over, was trapping that halliard against its cleat also.

The main topsail halliard must have been foul of the jammed foresail sheets also, because I remember being helpless to lower any sail at all as we rushed toward the stern of a pilot boat in the channel ahead. Darwin, not used to sail handling, had sensibly kept out of the way to avoid giving me any more problems. Unfortunately the only place he could stand was directly in front of Vicki, who was going frantic as she tried unsuccessfully to peer over or around his large form.

Somehow I finally freed the foresails, dropped the mizen topsail, the harassed Vicki having managed to sheet it in whilst steering and trying to see past Darwin, then dropped the mizen; its engulfing folds finally blocking Vicki's vision completely, but only slightly muffling her voice as she expressed her opinion of us both.

With the mainsail down and stowed, the diesel ticking over and Vicki's sight, if not her good temper, restored, the next part should have been easy. Only now the yacht club was suddenly ahead of us; the wind in our bare rigging now being strong enough to drive us inexorably toward the pontoons. No trouble, full astern on the diesel and "WHAT red light?!!!" Diana was pointing at the engine warning panel.

The water pump impeller had sheared off and the engine was rapidly overheating. Forward hastily to untie and let go the anchor, as a chorus of a million or so Arab onlookers, not knowing our reasons, screamed and gesticulated for us not to anchor but to come alongside. However, with a long seafaring tradition behind them, the Arabs were a lot quicker on the uptake than their equivalents in some other places in the world. Soon ropes were passed, order prevailed, and we were brought gently and securely to our proper place.

With the possible exception of Australia I know of no other country which makes such a performance of the simple formality of clearing in. And yet it is only fair to realise that the Egyptians have suffered several short but devastating wars in their recent history. Naturally they are security conscious. However, despite the number of officials involved, our business was transacted with pleasantness and goodwill all round.

We had heard much in our lifetimes of the habit of demanding "Baksheesh" and wondered if this would be another custom with which we must become familiar. All save one of the officials had departed, forms filled in and dues paid. The remaining one lingered, studying the interior of the boat. "Tact" said Vicki, "is not my strong point. I shall simply ask if he is waiting for money." She turned to the official and asked "Should we offer you baksheesh?" He paused a moment, looking carefully at the boat, at the children, at us. He smiled a gentle smile. Then he spoke. "No, lady" he said softly, "you need it more than me."

Strictly speaking we were not actually in Port Said; the yacht club is in Port Fuad, on the opposite side of the canal. The two towns are linked by a free ferry and thence I departed, once officially free to come and go, in search of the elusive water pump spares. Well, I expected them to be elusive, so it was a shock to see hanging out over the street a large illuminated "Yanmar Agent" sign. It couldn't be that easy; but it was.

The manager, taking his siesta on the office couch was perfectly happy to be disturbed, indicating a whole shelf of impellers and selling me two. I congratulated him on his excellent English. "Well old chap" he said, "I went to Reading University, you know." And returned to his nap.

Our canal transit was arranged easily through the good offices of Mr Bairam, of the Suez Canal Publicity department. A one time naval liaison officer, a cultured and much travelled man, also speaking impeccable English, he entertained me in the comfort of his air conditioned office; whilst a taxi driver, for the vast sum of three Egyptian pounds, took our papers from office to office until, after about three hours, all was in order.

The actual transit of the canal is rather dull in a small boat. The banks are barren sand, too high to see over. There was a mild diversion when our pilot for the second part of the journey, from Ismailia to Suez, developed amorous designs on Vicki, whom he pursued about the boat. His room to manoeuvre was restricted however, by the smallness of "Dorothy Ann", and his designs were easily thwarted when Vicki took refuge behind me. We speculated on what past successes might have encouraged him, as other skippers steered their boats down the long, hot reaches of the canal.

He further broke the monotony, and the mizen crosstrees, by unexpectedly trying to round up alongside an Italian yacht at Suez. The other boat was of massive all steel construction and quite unaffected. We came to rest in a shower of fenders, dan buoys and other objects stripped or thrown from our rails. The Italians, unharmed and amused, collected our belongings as we tied up; bringing us iced beer and producing ice cream for the children.

The next arrivals form a good illustration of the sort of confusion which the inexperienced Western traveller is bound to experience in the East. Two presentable young men, bearing enormous government forms, they were assumed by us to have official status. Many officials in Arab lands wear no recognisable uniform, although their status is apparently obvious to even the most ill educated Arab. In this case the young men were sons of "Prince of the Red Sea", this being the modest title of one of the local yacht agents. I have no idea, since we had, so far as we knew, attended to all the formalities of entry in Port Said, whether this further form filling was necessary. Once done and handed back to the young men though, we had employed the services of the agent and could expect to be charged accordingly.

In fairness to the Prince, whom we rather liked, he did in fact perform many small services for us and his command of English was invaluable. He arranged a car and driver to take us into Cairo; obtained malaria tablets, vegetables, diesel, making no charge for either the service or the goods themselves. Finally, he drove me through the swirling mass of Arab travellers who flow night and day through the Port of Suez, avoiding endless queues of whose purpose I was totally ignorant and leading me past the crowds to a quiet office, where my business was transacted easily in a few moments. On that day alone, he earned his fee of 90 Egyptian pounds.

Pyramids and Sphinx viewed, camels ridden and "Gyppy Tummy" A.K.A. "Montezuma's Revenge" contracted, it was time to go. The Italians were heading north for home at 5 a.m. so we had to release our lines to let them out of their position between us and the dock. There seemed little point in tying up again for only a few hours, so we set off at that time as well, south across Suez bay.

The bay, into which the canal debouches, lies at the head of the Gulf of Suez, a narrow, hazardous stretch of about 200 miles, which must be negotiated before entering the Red Sea. As we motored across its placid surface our stomachs became increasingly unhappy at the presence of some alien bacteria, demanding increasingly frequent use of our limited toilet facilities.

Our usually efficacious treatment for such disorders is to fast entirely for three days, as soon as symptoms are felt. This is more comfortable and gets results, but it leaves us too weak to work the boat properly. So we ate and hoped for the best, but to no avail. Finally we anchored for two days, behind our first ever coral outcrop, near the western shore. We recovered quickly, only to lose our main anchor, which had become so firmly jammed into the bottom that instead of it breaking free as the chain was hauled short in a choppy sea, the shackle holding anchor to chain was literally torn apart.Remembering some sound advice from Bob and Nancy Griffiths' classic cruising book "Blue Water", we had stocked the boat with five anchors. Having already lost two, we began to wonder if that was enough!

Hurried on our way, through a maze of shipping and

oil rigs, by a howling sandstorm, we thankfully reached the wider waters of the Red Sea. Catherine, set an essay to write for her school work, described the passage through the Gulf of Suez.

"Sandstorm in the Gulf of Suez"

By Catherine Jones Age 11

On the evening of the 18th June we had just passed Ras Gharib, half way down the Gulf of Suez. I found it scary and exciting when all at once the sky turned a sullen yellow; visibility decreased rapidly to only a few yards. It started to blow furiously and the air was thick with sand. Mummy called Daddy and he fought and struggled to get the main off, then he went to sleep as it was his watch below.

We had two oilrigs up ahead of us in the shipping lane. They were obliterated, lights and all. As we approached them the first ship of the convoy from the canal overtook us. We passed by one rig and could see two others standing close by.

"Kate!" I heard Mummy calling me out to help her, her voice shrill and anxious in the gloom. When I got out there I had to look for lights. Twenty minutes later I spotted lights like pinpricks piercing the murky yellow horizon.

"Lights to port."

"OK." Mummy checked her course; looked astern and then at the light up ahead. The light was a gas burnoff flare and I also saw a short stump (a well head) with a light on it. Then everything quietened down and I went to bed.

When I woke up we were approaching Ashrafi Reef, a coral reef only a few feet out of the water. It was not yet dawn and we wanted to pass in daylight, so somehow we had to slow down because with the sails up we were doing six knots which was far too fast – but we only got down to 4 knots under bare poles. As day broke we saw the slim finger of the lighthouse on the reef, whose light had guided us so far.

Some hours later we closed Shaker Island and we were through the Straits of Gubal; now to begin our 1,000 mile trip down the Red Sea.

In summer the wind is favourable for the southerly passage down the entire length of the Red Sea, so we had an uneventful 18 day voyage to Aden, in the South Yemen.

Aden offered an example of the utter simplicity to which entry proceedings can be reduced, if bureaucracy can be overcome. A simple, sensible form for the harbourmaster, another for immigration; ten questions in all and the reason for each obvious, then, within two hours of arrival, we were all free to go ashore.

With its long history of British occupancy, Aden has preserved some curious monetary terms from the old Empire. Although the official coinage is the Dinar, divided into 1,000 Fils, we had been forewarned that the locals reckoned in Shillings and Annas, a splendid Anglo Indian mixture. A further refinement of preserved English slang was revealed to me in the market one day. I was contemplating buying some melons displayed on a stall. Unusually, the stallholder spoke no English and I was having difficulty finding out the price. A jet black, semi naked figure, recumbent on the next stall, rose on one elbow, drawled in an impeccable British accent "They're ten bob, old boy" and lapsed back into his slumbers.

For those unversed in Early British currency, the conversion goes:

Ten bob = ten Shillings. One Shilling is 20 Fils. Therefore ten bob = 200 Fils. There are 1,000 Fils to the Dinar, which is worth about two quid (oops, sorry, £2). So a melon costs one fifth of 200p, which is 40p. I decided not to buy one.

There were other delights, the old beggar lady, dressed all in black, dragging herself in a sitting position the length of the bus floor as she collected alms, then smiling to display a fortune in gold teeth. The other Arab ladies who peremptorily tapped the nearest male on the shoulder when no seat was free, taking his seat, then handing him their ticket to punch, in the machine clipped to some far off pillar.

If I stood for a lady, several men would immediately offer me their seats. A visitor clearly could not be allowed to stand. Money carelessly dropped in the public market was returned to me. People approached us, politely, in the streets, to practise and display their English.

It is a poor country, except for the revenue of its great harbour, but rich in kindness and courtesy. Perhaps we noticed this more because we expected resentment, from the days when British rule was only overthrown by bitter fighting. We found none and when we enquired the charge for mooring the harbour staff laughed. "With those great vessels out there" they said, pointing from the windows of the control tower, "why would we need to charge for your little ship?"

We left with the South West Monsoon well developed. It was a deliberate choice as "Dorothy Ann" needed a strong wind to make good speed and our next stop was Sri Lanka, over 2,000 miles away across the Indian Ocean. The seas were moderate in the shelter of the Gulf of Aden, but once out of the lee of the Horn of Africa, as we passed well north of the island of Socotra, the waves became very large.

We were now in range of the B.B.C. World Service once again. Our pleasure at this was somewhat dampened when the first news which we received was of civil unrest in Sri Lanka. Once out of the gulf and in the grip of the monsoon there could be no going back, we were committed to our destination.

For two weeks we had winds of gale force, with sails constantly wet for half their height from flying spray. Then it slowly eased to lighter and lighter airs, until all our largest sails were set once more. In the evening, we noticed, at about 6 p.m. there would appear a few clouds and a squall or two would develop. After an hour or so they would die away, but having taken the large sails down in plenty of time we would leave them down until the next morning. Thus at midday Vicki, typically, was demanding more sail set, whilst I protested that we had too much up already if anything went wrong. "But look at it," she said, "hardly any wind and not a cloud in the sky. Well, excepting that tiny little thing over there." It was indeed a tiny cloud, as it rose into sight and drifted gently toward us, until it was overhead.

Then all hell broke loose. The sails filled, strained and heeled us violently. "She'll never stand this," I yelled, thinking of broken bowsprits and blown out sails as I tugged at the tiller line. The only snag with our self steering, at that early stage in its development, was that the line was knotted around the tiller, preventing large, rapid movements to windward.

Before I could undo the knot; before, probably, I could have borne away downwind to ease the strain, even with the tiller free, the mainmast broke. It was not at all violent. The cap moved so gently and yet inexorably forward, the spar pivoted slowly just above the crosstrees and then the broken 12 ft stub, hanging from a tangle of rigging, was flailing just above the deck.

I grabbed the swinging spar, fearful of the damage it might do, and swung mightily on the end of it for several moments, until I managed to rope it to a cleat. The wind had passed as quickly as it came, leaving us rolling becalmed on the chop it had raised on the water. It took us several hours to recover the sails, undamaged, from the water, get the broken spar untangled and roped down, devise a jury rig for setting on the stump of the mast and tidy away the upper rigging for future re-use.

Our large gaff mizen was back in service on its new boom so, with enough sail set forward to balance the boat, we could continue without much problem. We would have difficulty in going to windward, even more so than normally, though. It was this which finally decided us against a tentative plan for a stop at the Maldives en route, as it seemed safer to stay on the direct, downwind, track to Sri Lanka.

We reached Galle, on the southern coast of Sri Lanka,

28 days after leaving Aden, no more than two days later than we would have expected had the mast not broken. Formalities there are not onerous, but nothing much happens until initiated by the arriving skipper.

We tried to find out in advance, from a great number of sources, what procedure was required in each port. In some places setting foot ashore without clearance is totally forbidden. In others it is essential. In San Francisco it was necessary to take the whole family on the bus, over the Golden Gate Bridge and into the downtown business area, to clear in. In Australia no one must board or leave the vessel until the port doctor has been aboard and completed his inspection.

In Sri Lanka we knew that the law required us to have an agent. Knowing this, we had further been advised, luckily by a yacht's crew who had been there, to use Don Windsor, at Galle, rather than going into Colombo as we had first planned. We had written to Don, who had agreed to act for us, but didn't know if he would come to us, or we to him. In a harbour such as Galle, which always has moored yachts in it, there is a well tried system of obtaining more information. You shout. If you are an American and have not been to sea long enough for it to fail, you use the radio. But shouting is fine and doesn't need batteries either.

As a result of our shouting we learned that the port doctor would be coming to clear another yacht and would be told about us also. She duly arrived, aboard a harbour launch twice the size of our vessel, and went through the formalities. Then we were free to go ashore to the police station at the harbour gates, where immigration clearance was soon granted. That in turn left us altogether free to go where we would, ashore, though permitted only to anchor our boat in the harbours of Jaffna, Colombo, Galle, Trincomalee, or I think, Batticaloa. Anchorage anywhere else in Sri Lankan waters was, for no known reason, forbidden.

Don Windsor's house was nearby, offering showers, laundry, food and beer; not necessarily in that order. Don, a great man in the local community, with a soft spot for yachties, can do, get or fix anything. Or rather he always knows someone who will. His part is to sit on his verandah dispensing chat and hospitality, observing the world's frailties with a knowing but sympathetic eye.

We were three months in Sri Lanka, during which time we arranged for our mast repair, did a little touring and enjoyed Dengue fever and various stomach upsets. Delightful though some aspects of Sri Lanka are, it is the sort of place which makes one very grateful to have been born elsewhere. An air of "third world" slowness and inefficiency is apparent, though strangely, since its citizens are clever and hard working in the main. It seems that the western passion for order and neatness is not shared by most African and Asian people. I was disturbed to find that our travels, far from making us more understanding and sympathetic toward people of other lands, were inclined to produce feelings of national superiority.

Happily these feelings were quickly expunged by our experiences on our return to England. Apart from the shoddiness of our cities and schools, seen more clearly after a long absence than when observed day by day, we found ourselves dealing with officialdom. The discovery that the social benefits accrued over 30 years of work are entirely wiped out if one has the temerity to leave the country for a short spell is not pleasing. The arrogance, incompetence and disinterest shown by British officialdom is the equal of any in the world; we simply don't come into as much contact with it in the normal way. To be brought down a peg or two must though, however unenjoyable at the time, be a good thing for us in the long run.

That discovery was a long way in the future. Now we had parcels to collect, these being retained in the Post Office Customs department, at Colombo.

Colombo is some 70 miles from Galle, the general consensus of opinion being that the train offered the most comfortable journey thence. Only one snag. After numerous people had foregathered at the station next morning, it transpired that the train would not be appearing that day. Just why that should be was not explained. Indeed, it seemed that asking at all was not only obviously futile, but slightly infra dig as well. Only simple minded foreigners, it seemed to be implied, would waste time on such foolish questioning of the ways of railways.

This brought about our introduction to the minibus. An enlightened government, from which our own could learn much, had, despite its deficiencies, performed a stroke of genius in this field. By allowing tax relief on profits invested in the purchase of public transport vehicles, it had caused almost every Sri Lankan small businessman to form a bus company. Or so we were told. Certainly the place teemed with tiny buses, each crammed with twice its rated capacity of passengers and having more clinging to the outside.

Such buses were to be found in abundance in a parking area directly opposite the station. Locating the correct one was made easier by the crews, who stood alongside their vehicles shouting out their destinations. No matter that the first was full, another stood behind, ready to leave as soon as it was overloaded (if I may borrow a phrase from Anthony Smith). Thus we were transported to Colombo, in the space of a mere two and a half hours, for 14 rupees per person; about 50p.

The procedure at the Post Office was a model of such procedures the world over. Not, by any means, a model to be emulated by choice; an archetype rather, a distillation of the essence, the epitome of officialdom at its disinterested but obstructive best. Above all, a veneration of the principle of the queue.

There were, in all, five queues, the essential principle of anonymity being carefully guarded, to ensure that one stood for the maximum time in any one queue before discovering that it was necessary to occupy one or more others first. There were documents to hand in; others to collect; the ceremonial public opening of each parcel, with casual strewing and display of contents, of no importance in the case of our charts and spares but possibly embarrassing for a number of the Sri Lankan ladies, some of whose parcels contained gifts of a more intimate nature.

A bizarre part of the procedure was the need to glue form "A" onto form "B", using the contents of a dribbling and sticky pot provided for that purpose. Of course the unversed, such as we, queued to hand in form "A" before attaching form "B", thus needing to be loudly and publicly instructed in the correct procedure, before returning to spend the correct periods of waiting in their ordained sequence. There was, naturally, a queue for the glue pot.

Can these things arise by accident or simple default, or is there a world conspiracy by governments to keep people mindlessly occupied in queues, lest they have time and energy for insurrection and overthrow of the greedy and incompetent? No, on reflection it seems these things are simply the product of the small minded and uncaring. Poor Sri Lanka has the queues and insurrection as well.

This amazing performance was required of us whenever a parcel arrived, although ships' stores in transit, which ours always were, are free of duty. There was no "hassle", no attempt to extort money, for either official or unofficial reasons. Just a long, weary, pointless, time wasting rigmarole. We couldn't even get angry with the Customs men, they were far too pleasant and polite.

Time, both enemy and ally of the traveller, passed. Our repairs advanced. Items went for galvanising. Reese's anchor, from "Unlikely VII", was returned from the galvanisers in Colombo, sawn in half and reassembled with a large bolt through the shank. "Oh sir," the explanation ran, "it would not fit into the galvanising tank." We revised our policy, hastily recalled our own items and settled for rust retarding paint.

An excursion inland, for one packed week, travelling by public minibus, except for occasional flirtations with the State run Red buses where no minibus was available, provided many memories of a varied character. Hotels sans plumbing, apparent jam puffs concealing concentrated masses of curry stuffing, endless cups of tea made with condensed milk, photographing a wild leopard from a distance of 10ft or so, after borrowing the cash for the wildlife park entry fee from our taxi driver, thumbing an elephant ride in the street and riding home from a Kandian dance display with the dance troupe in their bus, are just a few which come to mind.

For these things and many more we have to thank the gentle, generous people of Sri Lanka, the "Beautiful Land". And when we read accounts by others, who have driven across the country by motor car, booked their entertainments from a travel agent and eaten in "tourist" restaurants, we feel vastly superior. Not only did we spend hours enjoying the company of whole bus loads (and overloads) of Sri Lankan people; it was also amazingly cheap; a factor which always counted heavily in our planning.

Our onward voyage to Sabang, the Indonesian free port on the tiny island of Weh, north of Sumatra, was made memorable by one thing only. Length. Delayed past the end of the favourable South West Monsoon by the need for the mast repairs, we took 42 days for a journey of 900 miles. For a while we felt that this might be some reflection on our ability, but the discovery that Tim Severin, no less, had taken 50 days over this same journey made us feel much better.

Our problem was not merely lack of wind, but a vigorous ocean current which sweeps southward through the Bay of Bengal, curves round the southern coast of Sri Lanka, then heads more to the west and the Maldive islands. We wanted to go toward the east, so plainly, with no wind with which to overcome it, we needed to escape the current. This we eventually did by edging our way, puff by scarce puff, to the southward, 240 miles, to where the Equatorial Counter Current flows toward the Sumatran coast.

The much thumbed weather charts and "Ocean Passages for the World" once more proved their worth. The currents were there as advertised and bore us silently and mysteriously on our way. Nearing Sumatra at last, as we realised from the presence overhead of that well known natural phenomenon, aeroplanes, the current trended toward the south, but by then we had wind enough to plod the 240 miles back northward to the latitude of Pulau Weh.

Christmas came as we crashed about in fickle winds and overfalls on the last few dozen miles of this leg. Reminded of my duty, I produced, in soaring galley temperatures, four pounds of Christmas pudding, all of which disappeared in record time. The monotony of the long passage was further broken by the engine governor spring fracturing. This brought us to a dead stop as we crossed the crowded shipping lane leading to the Malacca Straits, in a solid tropical downpour, at night; shortly after which the exhaust pipe set fire to the after bulkhead.

The deity which ensures that Catherine's birthdays are spent ashore then took over and we arrived calmly in Sabang without further mishap. Thanks to the frequent tropical squalls which we had experienced on the way we had, on this our longest lasting single journey, more water aboard on our arrival than we had on leaving the last port.

The Indonesian Immigration officer explained that, as we had neither visas nor Cruising Permit, we could stay only two days. There was however provision for boats to carry out necessary repairs; clearly, after a voyage of such length, many things would need attention. If I would just write a letter SO, saying THUS and THUS, he could then consider allowing us to stay longer. It was duly done, but he was greatly disappointed when I asked only for a one week stay, as we had to press on to Singapore before the winds failed us altogether. He was a most hospitable soul and an entertaining one, a free-fall parachutist with over 350 drops to his credit; one of which had ended in a serious arm injury, without in any way reducing his enthusiasm. We were invited to his home, taken out to dinner, driven in the government jeep, the three children bouncing around on him in the front seat, to an outdoor puppet show.

Dodent, a semi official yacht agent, took us to his

home, exchanged our books, took us to the swimming pool, brought our fuel and organised our laundry. Whatever commission he charged for these services was so low as to be undetectable. Our week passed very pleasantly indeed and all too soon it was time to go.

The wind, with fine perversity, now blew strongly out of the Malacca Straits, which was exactly where we wished to go. Unable to make headway against it we bore away on a long tack to the northeast. This brought us almost to Phuket, in Thailand, which was frustrating as we had originally planned to visit there and now, because of our previous slow passage, had insufficient time. As usual, persistence eventually got results and we made our slow way down the straits having, on one occasion when we bothered to count, had the lights of 75 vessels in sight at one time. In the local fashion there were many others no doubt, showing no lights at all.

Singapore, a confusing but not confused mass of shipping, oil rigs, land reclamation and construction work, was like nothing seen before. Singapore city breathes out energy. Its destination may be unclear but its velocity is apparent to all. Crowded and desirable, this island state carefully controls the comings and goings of outsiders.

An unwelcome restriction was the issue of visas for two weeks only. Further two week extensions are normally granted to those able to show possession of 5,000 Singapore dollars per person; not a fortune for a single traveller, but for five people with "only one wallet", as our friend Max once put it, not very practical. Even if we were prepared to lose the interest on it, £10,000 is more than I care to carry in my pocket. For the yachtsman wishing to refit, as we did, there is another option. Proof of work being carried out can be furnished to the port captain's office, together with a letter requesting an extension of stay. The port captain, once assured that genuine refitting is taking place, stamps the letter to indicate that he is satisfied that the application is justified, the letter is taken to immigration and another two weeks' stay is approved.

"I can't finish all this in two weeks" I said, "why can't I ask for a month?"

"Immigration only give two weeks" said the port office man. "Well I might as well ask" I said, and wrote accordingly. The port captain stamped the letter. I took it to immigration, they stamped our passports for a further month without question or comment and another myth was disproved. What is more, we did it twice.

Garbage dues were another hazard to the unwary. These were payable in advance at the port captain's office and were for a fixed period. Thus if one arrived just before the end of the period, the full amount for that period was still payable. The real catch though was that if one failed to pay in advance, the daily rate was charged and that was much greater. We had been warned in advance; also we were given written notice of the rules at the port captain's office, but it seemed that it had not always been so, leading to much upset and anger in the past.

We were to find that other countries had their idiosyncracies also. Australia, though making no charge for entry, demanded 35 dollars per person just for the paperwork to consider extending our visas, regardless of whether the extension was granted or not. They also demanded 40 dollars a head "departure tax" on each of the crew, whom they insisted in classing, insultingly we felt, as "passengers". There are no passengers on a small ocean going yacht and it seems that Australia is the only country unaware of the fact.

In Australia and even otherwise easy going New Zealand, one is virtually escorted from the premises the moment clearance out is granted. America will not even consider granting entry unless a visa has been issued prior to reaching U.S. territory; though the visa is issued readily and has no automatic expiry date. They charge for entry, visa extensions and clearance out, but not on the Australian scale. Clearance out is relaxed and one is not hustled away with unseemly haste.

Tiny Aitutaki, in the Cook Islands of the South Pacific, charges for Agriculture inspection, Customs clearance, mooring fees and a 20 dollar a head departure tax. However, they are friendly, generous, welcoming and have few sources of income. It is only when making a short stay that such charges seem excessive.

None of these variations of procedure cause much upset in English speaking countries, simply because they can be explained, however unjustifiable they may be. I do wonder though who invented the singularly stupid practice of charging people tax as they are leaving, when they may be expected to have used up or changed all their local currency. Why on earth not collect on their arrival, when at least they are likely to have the cash and can adjust their spending to allow for the deficit?

9
Down Under

One piece of officialdom which completely defeated us was the requirement for an Indonesian cruising permit. The state of Indonesia stretches from Malaysia and the Philippines in the north to Australia in the south. It has Sumatra for its western boundary and occupies half of New Guinea in the east. Most importantly from our point of view, it claims all the sea within that area as its territorial waters and requires all vessels to obtain a cruising permit before entering the area. We had heard the usual mixture of stories of applications refused, bribes taken, payments of several hundred dollars to "agents" being made with no results forthcoming. By the time we reached Singapore the political situation in Indonesia had deteriorated and rumours were rife.

It usually pays to find out the rules and follow them, although sometimes information is difficult to obtain outside of the particular country. We had planned to apply from Singapore rather than from England, reasoning that it was closer both in time and distance; the Indonesian embassy in Singapore though, was unable to help.

Indonesia is ruled by the Javanese, who occupy all the positions of power and importance in all the multitude of islands which make up the country. This arrangement is not universally popular and leads to frequent outbreaks of civil strife. Our impending arrival coincided, although we were not aware of it until much later, with a particularly violent upheaval in Irian Jaya, the Indonesian half of the island of New Guinea. The advice of the embassy officials was to fly down to the capital, Jakarta, and apply there. There was no difficulty in obtaining a visa for travel by air. We were not at all sure of the wisdom of this however, as the air fare of 80 dollars was a substantial outlay and there was no guarantee that the permit would be issued or any certainty that payment, reasonable or otherwise, might not be required.

The clinching argument was produced by some Italian friends, operating a charter boat out of Singapore to the Indonesian archipelago. They told us that possession of a cruising permit did not automatically confer a right to travel anywhere in the area. Indonesian patrol boats guard the many areas where there is political upheaval and will direct cruising yachts elsewhere. That would probably result in our being unable to sail out through the eastern part of the archipelago as we wished. We decided that we could probably sail down past Sumatra and out through the Sunda strait into the Indian ocean without trouble, particularly as "Dorothy Ann" was not very different looking from the local sailing craft, which still ply all the way into Singapore. We could then go via Christmas Island and Fremantle to Adelaide, instead of our alternative of Brisbane, Sydney, Adelaide. We would not land anywhere in Indonesia, but would make passage direct to Christmas Island, which is an Australian territory.

And so we set off again, well laden with extra fuel for the diesel engine, as we were expecting light winds and calms for the first part of the passage. Quite a fresh breeze carried us on our way south from the sea lanes around Singapore, as we left with with many a cheery wave from the Singaporean patrol boats which guard those waters. Soon we were passing between the first group of islands to the east of Sumatra, where we anchored overnight as there are no lights in those confined waters.

The following days brought the expected light winds, but not too light to make progress. We were glad, especially at night, not to travel too fast, as there were quite a lot of trees floating in the water which, although fairly light, frond padded, palm trees, still caused quite a thump and a rattle as we collided with them from time to time, in the darkness.

We rigged a canvas awning over the cockpit and relaxed beneath its shade as we made our slow way down to and across the equator. The usual ceremonies were observed, with King Neptune lathering and shaving the crew, using a rope's end for a brush and a glittering cardboard and tinfoil razor, cunningly fashioned during the night watches. Mrs Neptune got rough though, dumping a bucket of seawater over the unsuspecting king's head.

After an uneventful passage we reached the first obstacle, in the form of a string of oil rigs across our path. The chart shows oil rigs, of course, but cannot show every individual one, especially where there is such a proliferation of them as in this case. It also shows such things as the unswept World War II minefield, which occupies a vaguely defined position adjacent to the rigs. The problem which we faced was that the oil rigs had spread westward toward the minefield for such a distance that our simple plan of sailing between them and the mainland was impracticable. There must clearly be an accepted way between them, but where? For safety reasons all countries have restrictions on unauthorised craft passing in close proximity to rigs and, with no cruising permit, we had no desire to draw attention to ourselves by a breach of the rules. The problem was solved in the simplest manner imaginable, when a small ship steamed slowly into sight, passed between the rigs and disappeared over the horizon astern of us. We had observed its track and simply sailed in the reverse direction. No one bothered us and that night we had the flaming beacons of the gas burn off flames, still visible behind us, to guide us on our way.

Next day Krakatoa was in sight, smoking steadily as it builds a new volcano to replace the old. The chart carried a notation "Underwater volcanic activity; avoid this area." So far as we could determine we were slowly drifting to and fro over the indicated spot, the wind having at last failed, at the whim of each tide. Unwilling to burn diesel fuel unless we really had to, in case of further calms when we were far from land, we continued to drift uneasily in the same area for two days. Apart from a faint smell of sulphur though, nothing alarming happened.

We eventually slid out through a narrow, rock fringed channel between Java and a large island at its western end. That was exciting because there was only one light visible to guide us, we had violent squalls with blinding rain in the darkest hours of the night, then at dawn we were becalmed again on an immense swell which was bent on carrying us ashore. Now, as we looked at the cliffs only two wave troughs away from us, we were very glad indeed that we had conserved our fuel. I just hoped that the motor would continue to run; a concern which tends to be acute with single cylinder motors. It did. It was the sort of gentlemanly motor which only breaks down where repair facilities are at hand, or when there is at least plenty of sea room.

Once we were safely clear of the land the wind returned, speeding us on our way toward Christmas Island at a welcome and unexpected pace. Soon Vicki faced her first real challenge as a navigator. The island is only a few miles across; beyond it, 3,500 miles of empty ocean stretch away to Antarctica. Australia is 900 miles away to the eastward, with winds and current both unfavourable for an approach from the northwest. It is no place to be lost.

The great day came, when we were deemed to be within sighting distance. "Can you see it yet?" came the voice from below, where herself was busy at the chart table. "Nothing in sight so far," I replied, scanning the horizon busily. The navigator bustled out of the hatch, armed with a hand bearing compass and looked along her calculated bearing. "Well, it's there where it ought to be," she said scornfully, and immediately retreated below once more. Sure enough, there was a faint grey conical shape which I had missed at first, right on the correct bearing.

The sea around the island is deep; so deep that even large vessels cannot anchor, but tie to buoys anchored to a small coral ledge close inshore. In bad weather, or if another vessel is already moored, the ship must lie off, drifting and returning until mooring is possible. This caused us a worried night because, as we approached the island through a chain of squalls, we could see the lights of a ship under way, but could make no sense of her course. Also, she seemed to get closer and then recede. She was, of course, standing off and waiting to moor.

We arrived the next morning in a blinding downpour; being "talked in" to a good position, over the V.H.F. radio, by the marine superintendent on the island. Clearance was swift and easy, in the capable hands of Kathy the cop, an Australian lady police sergeant who dealt with our documents and made us coffee with the same casual efficiency. "Do you come from Australia?" the girls asked her. "You're in Australia now," Kathy replied with a grin. And so we were as, invited to use the facilities of "The Boat Club", we revelled in the exotic and unaccustomed luxuries of microwaved steak pies and chilled Fosters lager.

We had planned to stay for three days; inevitably it was suddenly Easter and, "Oh dear, shame," etc. we were forced to spend more time lazing on the beach and snorkelling over our first visible coral, instead of fighting our way south toward Fremantle. Vicki was born on 13 April; now she was able to send a telegram to her parents: "Arrived Christmas Birthday. Leaving Easter."

As an anchorage it had its bad points. Being a wide bay, completely unprotected from the north, it would be necessary to get out quickly if the wind came from that quarter. Even when it didn't, there was a considerable swell most of the time. I had some work to do up the mizen mast, which necessitated tying the bosun's chair to the shrouds at all four of its corners, to prevent me from being beaten to death against the mast. That in turn made for very slow progress as I untied and re-tied my strings every few feet up and down.

The good news was that anchorage was free. We were surprisingly ignorant about mooring fees in general, except for an awareness that they were absurdly high in

England. One of the reasons why I had not owned a boat earlier was an extraordinary decision by the courts, when I was still in my twenties, to extend the rights of landowners to the centre of waters separating their properties, which had for centuries provided a free haven for small boats. Given such a licence to print money, the landowners reacted in the obvious manner by demanding exorbitant fees from the boat owners and putting the cost of keeping a boat instantly beyond the means of most of us.

We had finally found an answer by joining a group renting a stretch of tidal mudflat from the Crown. This provided a filthy and inaccessible, but relatively cheap, mooring site on which to put down one's own anchors and chain. From there, in our shallow boats, we had cruised the Essex rivers, becoming expert at finding other spots on the mud for our intermediate anchorages. Later we had moved to an equally cheap, and muddy, and filthy, club mooring; more accessible except when the local council, who presumably haven't heard about tides in the 800 years of the town's existence, lock the park gates leading to the moorings with a complete disregard for the times of high water.

Marinas, with their fees for a week in excess of our mooring charges for a year, were something to be avoided. With, mostly unused, boats jammed in by the dozen, it's like camping in a car park anyway. Since leaving England we had only used the marinas at Vila Moura, in Portugal, and in Gibraltar. Each had cost less than half as much as Newhaven in, I am ashamed to say, my own county of Sussex, and was worth it for the ease with which we could get ashore for showers and laundry. Oh yes, there was one other, our one day stay in Spanish Estapona, at a similar cost.

I don't remember the yacht club in Vigo charging us at all. Certainly I would expect foreign visitors to my own club to be given free mooring for a short stay. I always thought that was what yachting was all about. I was wrong. For most clubs it seems to be about rushing round a row of buoys in an ill mannered way each weekend and defending their moorings against all outsiders. It is always painful to have one's illusions destroyed; fortunately there is in this case a powerful reality to compensate for the loss.

The real romantics, unexpected and unlikely though they might seem at first glance, are the hard bitten professionals of the sea. That is why they are there. It is the fishermen, the merchantmen, the naval servicemen, the port officials, customs officers, any of the people who have chosen to work on or by the sea, who understand and sympathise with the cruising sailor. Not all, of course, but a very large number and their warmhearted support and often practical assistance more than makes up for the disinterest of the "yachting" community.

These are of course generalisations, with the danger of all such statements that they are more likely to harm the good exceptions than to be felt by the indifferent majority. Let us have no more of them, but see instead what specifically happened.

As we were leaving the anchorage at Christmas island the Yanmar diesel suddenly lost oil pressure. It was a sheer fluke that I was coming aft through the boat, facing the warning lamp panel as the red light came on. Sail was already hoisted and although we instantly stopped the motor we were getting just enough wind to steer clear of the ship mooring buoys and away from the island. We wouldn't really need the motor again before we reached Fremantle, so we decided just to carry on.

Our French friends Pierre and Brigitte, who were also heading for Australia in their 30ft steel sloop, soon drew well ahead of us, as we expected them to, and we were on our own again. This we had always expected to be the most difficult part of the trip. Adrian Hayter, in 1954, had a great deal of trouble reaching the Australian mainland at all; putting in eventually to Geraldton and having even more difficulty with the subsequent passage to Fremantle.

The weather charts were discouraging. We had picked a time of year when conditions were such as to make the journey merely difficult, rather than impossible, yet even then all the winds were forecast as blowing from south to north, with all the prevailing currents flowing that way too. A long slog, as close to the wind as we could sail, out to the southwest; then we should find the top edge of the great westerly airstream which flows, unobstructed by any land, around the southern part of the globe.

With the westerlies we could head east for Fremantle, this long, dog leg route, taking perhaps six weeks; much longer if any failure of sails or gear occurred. We had more than ample food stores aboard; our limitation was water, of which we had sufficient for 10 weeks at our normal rate of consumption. It would become obvious well in advance though if the need for rationing was going to arise, so we could last much longer if need be.

As far as the wind direction was concerned it was rather an anticlimax. We were able to lay a course almost due south at once; later the wind backed to become even more favourable, allowing us to head directly for Fremantle. It was strong too, so we kept up as much sail as we dared and roared along famously. But the journey was not without incident.

The first failure was the chain bobstay which parted, fortunately, when we had only the small jib set, so the strain on the bowsprit was not enough to break the spar. Somehow I managed to get a hook on the end of a new chain to go through the shackle at the waterline, despite it being submerged regularly to a depth of three feet or so. When this had been attached and tightened, the bowsprit firmly held down once more, I tackled the motor. Discovery number one had been that the oil pipe, cunningly designed to be at the lowest point and thus collect any salt water which landed anywhere on the motor, had rusted through. Discovery number two was that the stock of spare copper tubing, enough to replace, with no further risk of rusting, all the pipework on a dozen engines if need be, had gone into a box stored back in England.

I now attempted to roll a strip of sheet brass around the damaged part of the pipe and solder it in place. It only took two days! But it worked. Of course the batteries were flat by then, so we had to crank the diesel by hand, always an entertaining exercise. Finally, taking advantage of a burst of speed and leaving it in gear, so that I got some help from the prop, I managed to start it. The batteries soon charged up and we switched off, with everything in working order again.

I don't remember what kept me out on deck for a while that night; nothing very special, as I recall. When I went back below though there was a curious mistiness in the air. My first thought was that the stove had not been properly turned off and had somehow leaked warm paraffin vapour into the air; something which had happened once or twice before, but never in such quantity. I let the pressure out of the stove, then went out for a quick look around the horizon before investigating further. As soon as I glanced at the compass I realised that I was on the wrong track. The light was out. Back below then, to find that the batteries were not only flat, but too hot to touch. The starter cable had chafed on the side of the motor, shorted out, vaporised its insulation, then melted. It is the one cable which is not fuse protected, naturally.

When the wiring had been replaced we had, of course, to hand start the motor again. It didn't want to play this time and then the main peak halliard chafed through, letting the top of the mainsail down on deck in a crumpled heap. We had to drop the sail for a while, but when the wind moderated we used the topsail halliard to successfully reset it. By now we were nearing Fremantle, rising and falling on a huge swell, with crayfish pots scattered like mines across the surface of the sea. We rolled and heaved across the swell, weaving between the rows of pots, as I struggled to strip down and repair a defective diesel injector. There should have been a spare, a maintenance manual and other spares, but, though ordered, they had never arrived. Rather to my surprise my improvised repair worked. We cranked the motor, it fired, ran, and soon we were on the V.H.F. to the port office, asking where we should dock. The Fremantle Sailing Club sent a boat out to lead us in and officialdom in its many forms (and with its many forms) assembled on the dock to meet us. We had reached the Australian continent, the only objective which we had set ourselves.

We were made welcome in an offhand manner which was, I think, more a respect for our privacy, combined with a characteristic liking for getting on with their own affairs rather than other people's, which typifies many Australians, than any lack of interest or hospitality. Besides which we spent much of our time ashore, staying with Nevil and Shiona, old friends of Vicki's parents.

The club commodore, Norman Beurteaux, and his wife, came aboard to welcome us and we were invited to as many meals as we could possibly have eaten, by hospitable members. The question of mooring fees was, however, a subject of hot debate in the club at that particular time.

For three days there was no charge at all; this I think was not in question. The practice thereafter was to charge 10 dollars a day; rather more than most cruising budgets could sustain. An indignant member, whom we had met earlier in Sri Lanka, and who was agitating for no charge at all to be made, became almost speechless when one member apparently stated that visitors should not be encouraged because "They might use the hot water in the showers."

Personally I doubt if news of the availability of hot showers in Fremantle, though we used them gratefully enough, will create an unmanageable rush of foreign yachtsmen to selfishly consume the hot water. Our own immediate problem was solved simply by the club secretary, who pointed out that it was the last month of the current membership year. We could join for the balance of the year, then pay the members' rate for mooring. Thus we paid about 100 dollars for our one month's stay; a reasonable compromise.

The Fremantle Sailing Club really is a great club in a beautiful State. It would be a great shame if it becomes too expensive a base for the overseas visitor to rest and refit after the long haul south.

The children were collected by their grandparents and

borne away by bus, on a 36 hour drive across the Nullarbor desert, to Adelaide, in South Australia. They were quite happy to go; only rather concerned over our ability to manage the boat on our own. We assured them that, though it might be rather a struggle to cope alone, we would manage somehow. They were to attend school in Willunga and were looking forward to making more friends of their own age.

In fact we managed very well, rolling out of Fremantle on the same glassy swells which had greeted us on our arrival, with all sail set and hardly enough wind to fill them. Soon though we had wind to spare and were snugged down under our favourite rig of main trysail, mizen, small staysail and small jib. With this sail plan and a strong wind on the quarter we could, and did, fly.

An Irish freighter crossing the Great Australian Bight told us the windspeed was 45 knots. It increased later, so that we arrived in the Gulf of St Vincent doing a breathtaking eight and a half knots, having covered 1,340 miles in 13 days. We found ourselves off the port of Adelaide in the late evening. It was dark, intermittent rain squalls swept over us, the area north of the port is ill lit and dangerous, and we feared being driven that way if the wind further increased, which it was obviously doing.

Trying to find the way into the Port River and thence into the Royal Yacht Squadron, as we originally planned to do, seemed likely to prove difficult for strangers, in bad conditions and darkness. Entry to the new North Haven marina development at the river mouth looked possible though; our chart was new and the lights looked adequate. The snag was that it was dead downwind. Once committed to an approach it was very unlikely that, with our limited auxiliary power, we could turn back and get clear of the coast if for any reason we could not enter. We got all sail off and started in with the motor ticking over, doing four knots through the water from the windage of our rigging alone and surfing our 15 tons on top of the waves, which began to roll and break as the depths decreased. We followed the Port River lights easily to the point where the channel turns, then headed in on the compass course for the marina entrance, looking for the entrance lights.

We found the lights after a few anxious moments; the only snag was the solid wall stretching across between them. It really didn't do either my or Vicki's nerves any good at all to see it. There was no wall there on the chart, that was certain, as we scrutinised it minutely. Horrible memories of lights seen over walls when approaching from the wrong angle, on previous entries to other ports, rose up to alarm us. We could only resolve the mystery by approaching closely; then, if the entrance was not there, we would in all probability die. We didn't like it much.

When we were about a boat's length from the wall we saw the entrance, to port, where it had to be if it existed at all. The wall apparently across the entrance was a new breakwater; a very recent addition to prevent surge from entering the basin. Turning, we were soon bearing down on another wall at the end of the marina; we needed full power astern just to stop our headlong progress, for the wind inside was deflected by the walls and followed us still. Manoeuvring by inches, we edged our stern within range of a mooring pontoon. Vicki jumped down with a rope, made it fast, and we were safe. We finished mooring properly, went ashore and found a friendly security man. Yes, there was a telephone, and there, God bless him, were the showers! The wind speed indicator on the wall by the phone read 55 knots.

We phoned Vicki's parents, were collected next day and driven to their home in the almond-growing district of Willunga. The next four months were spent trying to be in Willunga and the North Haven at the same time; tricky, as they are 44 miles apart. Bill and Joan were still trying to settle into a house which they had only moved to a year before. Somehow they organised and coped with a 250% increase in their household without complaint. Bill spent long hours in his excellent workshop building and repairing a miscellany of boat's gear. Joan produced immense meals from her beloved garden, which she cultivates from dawn to dusk. Having given Vicki and me a trailer caravan in their garden, as our own private apartment, they saw little of us and much of the children. That was probably as it should be, but sometimes we felt that we were doing little to show our appreciation.

The commodore and members of the Cruising Yacht Club of South Australia (C.Y.C.S.A.), into whose private marina we had stumbled so precipitately in the dark, disproved all our preconceived notions about yacht club hospitality, overwhelming us with their interest and generosity. It was ironic to realise, in a very short space of time, that the Royal Squadron were equally hospitable, as was the Port Adelaide Sailing Club. The cruising sailor can depend on a warm welcome in Adelaide and he need not fear that excessive costs will curtail his visit there; the South Australians will "see him right", as Malcolm and Mike did for us and many more were willing to.

Our normal routine was to spend the weekdays at Willunga, though I would sometimes need to spend a day on the boat at midweek, all five of us returning on board from Friday evening to Sunday evening. We had, as always, work to do. Also we wanted to be at the C.Y.C.S.A. at weekends so that the members could visit "Dorothy Ann" and talk about cruising, if they wished. It meant that Bill and Joan got a break from the children once a week too, but it entailed an awful lot of driving, in the old Cortina which Bill had lent us. On our first Sunday evening we discovered one of those demented rulings to which local government is much addicted, this one being daft enough to be English. For some strange reason the city council, in its infinite wisdom, has decided that it is sinful to sell petrol to motorists on a Sunday evening. All unsuspecting and knowing that we had passed at least a dozen filling stations on our journey in through the city, we left the club late at night with a near empty tank. After driving, with increasing concern and puzzlement, past an infinity of dark and shuttered filling stations, we unknowingly reached the border of the prohibited area and were bewildered to see eight separate stations in a solid line, with all their pumps lit and doing a roaring trade. It was a relief, as we had been driving with the gauge on "empty" for some time and the Cortina was not an economical vehicle by any means. Nonetheless we were sad to realise that even Australian citizens can be forced to tolerate such pointless stupidity.

Apart from the flourishing weed of petty bureaucracy, which nobody in the world seems able to eradicate or even keep from spreading, we found Australia to be a wonderful country. The real problem for the visitor is the huge size of the continent, the enormous distances between the "settled areas" where the main cities are; miles of desert roadway with very little traffic in places. It is not a place for foolhardy adventures in old vehicles, so we were not able to see the interior during our stay. We were, in any event, hard put to find time for the many invitations to visit which poured in from all sides. We gave talks to the yacht clubs and to the Australian Volunteer Coastguard, which we hoped would repay a little of the debt of gratitude which we felt. The result was even greater displays of generosity, gifts and invitations, which left us completely overwhelmed.

There was the wonderful day spent partly with John and Mavis aboard "Oberon", then at the Port Adelaide Sailing Club, eating, drinking and listening to New Orleans style jazz, which is very much alive and well in Australia, to our great delight. And the evening with Lindsay and Mary, when we laughed till our sides ached; an evening which we longed to repeat, yet never found the time. But perhaps the highlight of them all was the evening spent with David and Liz.

It had a promising start when Vicki, with a faith in the "road" map more appropriate to Hampstead than the outer regions of Adelaide, directed me down a washed out gulley with a slope across its width which threatened to overturn the car at anything over a walking pace and a very slow one at that. Surviving this short cut, we located the correct driveway and fought the Cortina around its sinuous downward curves; mentally flinching from contemplating the ascent to come. Wonderfully organised, David and Liz banished our combined offspring to a room adequately supplied with food, fizzy drinks and television; from which they were unlikely to appear voluntarily. We adults were then plied with superb wine and food before settling down comfortably to compete in the telling of sailing stories. David won handsomely, leading with a story of an engine leaving its bearers right in front of the Royal Squadron's clubhouse and then capping that with a true yachtsman's tale of a distressed damsel, bad weather, tight jeans, basic plumbing arrangements and his own attempts to assist the maiden. It gained much from the physical re-enactment, which cannot be reproduced here. However he scored an overwhelming bonus when, asked how well he had known the young lady, he replied with a slow smile "Ah, er, intimately."

It was understandably late, or questionably early, when we said our goodnights and set off up the twisting climb to the road. It seemed as if some malign agency was resisting my attempts to turn one way and savagely wrenching the car around in the other. When we arrived in the road it soon became clear that there was indeed something very much wrong. Correcting a wild swerve on the very edge of the gutter I pulled up and got out. The front tyre was very flat. Also, the handle of the only jack in the car could not be rotated without hitting the body. Removing and re-positioning the handle every half turn made a slow job of changing the wheel, but eventually it was done. Heaving a sigh of relief I jumped in, accelerated away and discovered that we had a terrifying wheel wobble at 27 mph, which tore the steering wheel from my hands. It was now 3 a.m. and I had to drive unobtrusively across the whole of Adelaide, at less than 25 mph on virtually empty roads, if we were to avoid attracting police attention. It was now some time since I had drunk any alcohol, but being breathalysed is something I prefer to avoid even when sober. We made it, safely and unmolested, to the North Haven and the welcome security of "Dorothy Ann". It had certainly been a memorable evening.

One day, soon after our arrival, we received a letter

from a couple who were proposing to buy a cruising boat themselves in the near future. "Could we" they wrote, "help you in any way? We have transport, a house, tools and quite a lot of D.I.Y. experience, though we're not experts on boat work." Or words to that effect; their letter has gone the way of all our souvenirs. We hastened to accept their offer. Pat and Tony plunged into our work as if "Dorothy Ann" were their own boat. They washed sails (using their swimming pool for that purpose) scraped and varnished spars, cleaned, painted, sewed, mended, repaired and built, until the boat was transformed. As if that were not enough, they also fed and entertained us and sent us off with an immense box of surprise gifts which, opened one a week as Sunday treats, lasted until the end of the voyage. Pat, who for some reason became known as Mrs Pat, presumably to differentiate her from any lesser Pats who might be around, tackled the problem of our tea and coffee jars, which stood, unsecured, behind the galley sink. She designed and built a partitioned shelf which neatly held four jars, for tea, coffee, sugar and powdered milk, plus a few other items which had no proper stowage. Modestly she said "It will probably break or fall down and you'll say 'why on earth did she give us that bloody thing?'" From that day on it was always known as "Mrs Pat's Bloody Thing" though in fact it worked perfectly, was neat, unobtrusive and never in the least looked like breaking or falling down.

Vicki's only sister, Diana, had followed her parents to Australia and subsequently married an Australian. We had never met her husband, Nick, who had a reputation for not suffering fools gladly. Visiting them and their children, James and Kate, we were flattered to find that Nick seemed not to suffer very much in our presence, being in fact as pleasant, and hospitable a person as one could hope to meet, as well as extremely helpful. They have a farm, high in the hills above Willunga, where the children stayed to feed lambs and watch the kangaroos, testing Uncle Nick's tolerance well beyond all reasonable limits. I was able to take our dinghy there, to rebuild it in comfort in their big hay barn, whilst Diana and Nick fed and spoiled me, taking care that I didn't work too hard. We felt very secure and at home with them; leaving was unusually hard.

Other friends entertained us; John and Lesley, from the Royal Squadron, took us for a guided tour of Adelaide, their fellow members, Dick and Kay gave us a barbecue, following the luxury of a long wallow in their jacuzzi. Kay also gave us recipes for good things to cook at sea, and a huge tin box of examples to whet our appetites. We took a long drive to Murray Bridge where Bruce and Jane have their home. The journey was somewhat marred by the fact that we all had colds and the poor old Cortina was at last beginning to protest at the way it was being overworked in its old age, but the welcome which we received on our eventual arrival made the effort well worth while. Alan, another member of the Royal Squadron, who has voyaged across the globe, lent us any of his huge stock of charts which we cared to take. Other charts, always a major expense, were sent to us at the club by a donor who left, on travels of his own, before we could thank him.

On some weekends the children, according to their custom, went on travels of their own. As well as various excursions with "Uncle Nick and Auntie Di", they were taken away by friends Betsy and Max for various treats, including a long and enjoyable weekend visit to their property in Waikerie. So, as usual, they managed to see more of the country than we mere adults did.

Meanwhile, John and Lesley had taken away the name boards from the stern of "Dorothy Ann", which Lesley had offered to repaint. One day they appeared at the yard, with the boards wrapped in paper. "We've done them," said John, cheerfully and innocently. "It was 'Gertrude Mary', wasn't it?" Vicki's face fell and they hooted with laughter, as they unwrapped the boards to reveal "Dorothy Ann. Cardiff" neatly lettered in black, on a white background. Between us, "Dorothy Ann" became "Gertrude Mary" from that day onward.

September came, bringing the end of the southern

Winter. We arranged to take Nick, Diana, Pat and Tony for a brief day-sail, by way of thanks for their help. On the day the weather was ideal for our overcrowded vessel and we had a pleasant and relaxed trip, though the lack of wind made it rather unadventurous. We also arranged for Diana and Nick to spend a night on board, in the marina. This was a more limited success; the winter, though cold, had been dry enough to shrink the deck planks, creating some tiny leaks in the seams once more. Unknown to all of us, Nick was sitting under one of the leaks as rain began to fall onto the decks. As a stream of water suddenly descended on his head he leapt to his feet with a roar of "Oh.........POOP", which from then onward became the standard expletive used on board. Considering that he then spent the night with his tall body compressed into one of our short, narrow bunks, wrapped in crackling plastic as a precaution against further leaks, his good humour next day was incredible. Diana, almost as tall and kept awake by the crackle of plastic as Nick moved in his sleep, was less amused.

We timed our leaving to coincide with the C.Y.C.S.A.'s "opening day", the start of season celebration which the clubs hold annually. It was an accidental choice at first, but we decided to stick to it, reasoning that everyone else would be enjoying the festivities in the evening, whilst we slipped quietly away unnoticed, having privately said our goodbyes to the family earlier.

It was not like that at all. Betsy started it off, arriving in the afternoon with champagne. I don't remember who brought the beer; Ray, perhaps; I seem to remember that Merle brought food. So did John and Lesley; a whole bucket of Irish stew to reheat for our first meal at sea. Bruce and Jane appeared; so did more beer. We don't drink alcohol at all when at sea, nor, usually, when about to depart. Even on this occasion we only drank sparingly, but the increasing numbers of people and the effort to complete our preparations without ignoring anyone, have made it difficult to recall accurately just who came when, bearing what. Parties aboard nearby boats, having less cause for moderation (something which I have always believed should be practised in moderation) caroused with growing enthusiasm; singing began.

Late in the evening, much later than we intended, we finally squeezed our way through the crowd to say our goodbyes to commodore Malcolm Kinnaird and manager Jim Henry. With the singers well into "We'll meet again" John cast off our lines and walked us gently astern from the berth. To the strains of "Auld Lang Syne" we nosed slowly ahead; Merle, armed with camera and flashgun, was sprinting along the darkened pontoons and yelling "over here Josh" as she found a good camera angle.

The transition is always abrupt, always painful. Leaving is the real price which the traveller pays for his welcome. In a few minutes we were out of the glow of the marina lights, eyes straining to adjust to near total darkness, edging slowly out through the entrance channel. By the time we had grown used to the old familiar world of dark, glittering, heaving water, under faint starlight, the shore was already distant.

10
Paradise Found

Our next destination was the one place on earth at which Joshua Slocum said he was tempted to leave the sea and settle ashore; Devonport, Tasmania. First though we had to pass through "Backstairs Passage", between the mainland and Kangaroo Island. The wind was rising, giving our out-of-practice stomachs a great deal to think about. The demand for reheated Irish stew was not great, so I felt obliged to consume a large portion, just to show my appreciation of Lesley's kind gesture in preparing it for us.

There was an unsettled period that year, before the hot Summer weather became established. Our trip to Tasmania was wet and windy throughout, though we did get a couple of pleasant days at the very end of the journey. Through "Backstairs Passage" the wind blew hard from ahead and we scraped through, motor-sailing on a single long tack from close in to the mainland shore, just clearing the rocks to the south of Kangaroo Island. By the time the planks had swollen again to seal the decks tight, all our bedding was soaked with salt water once more. We had replaced the offending caulking compound on the fore and after decks, with red lead putty, which worked perfectly, but we never found the time for the major task of resealing the whole of the main deck.

A great event however took place during this time; we caught our first fish with hook and line. Apart from the three speared in the Indian Ocean, we had caught nothing, despite trailing lines and baits for thousands of miles. Now a small squid had the misfortune to land, as they often did, on deck. I put it on a hook, paid out the line and, to everyone's disbelief, it was taken by a barracuda. Not the world's finest fish, but good eating nonetheless.

Vicki summed it up in a letter to Lesley and John:

"Ugh! What a leg! Seasick and cold. I can't think why we do it!! Would you believe that our beautiful paint and varnish (we had left Adelaide with it all spotlessly renewed) looks as if it needs 'just a spot of attention'?! The sea makes a good sandpaper substitute."

As we motored at last up the Mersey river, looking for a place to moor, a car drove onto the quay and a figure jumped out, waving to us to come across to the side. It was Dick, the assistant harbour master, who invited us to tie up to the dredger for the night. We had to check in with customs before going ashore, but the harbour controller, going off duty, drove to the shop and brought milk and bread for us.

Once again it was time to clean and repaint the bottom; the last occasion having been when we beached for that purpose in Singapore. That had been sufficient for renewal of the antifouling paint, but now we needed to have time for a more thorough check and perhaps some recaulking or other attention. "Dorothy Ann" had been just too heavy for the marine railway at the C.Y.C.S.A. Here at Devonport were cradles capable of carrying much bigger boats, in the very place where Slocum had hauled out before the turn of the century. The haul out was quickly arranged; then we crossed the river to visit the yacht club. The commodore greeted us, told us we were welcome to lie alongside the club's pontoon, had a shower key provided for us and generally made us feel welcome. The effect was somewhat spoiled by the irate member who arrived at the boat next day, demanding to know what the devil we were doing in that spot, where he intended to moor his boat, and so on at some length. He finally gave us an opportunity to explain that we had been invited to visit, but didn't seem much mollified, grumbling that he had not been consulted. We were quite pleased that we were about to leave and go across to the slip anyway.

The slipways are located very near the main road bridge over the Mersey, in clear view of the traffic over the bridge. This, combined with the fact that we were interviewed by T.V., radio and two newspapers immediately after our arrival, caused us to be noticed. We had over 100 visitors to the boat in one week, many of whom brought gifts. Once again we were feted and feasted like heroes. Jake; artist, marine historian, printer and arch-wangler, sold a superb pen drawing of "Dorothy Ann" to pay our slipping costs. He also caused a very large quantity of stores to appear at the slip. They gave me a major stowage problem, but were still feeding us when we reached the U.S.A. Jenny and Hein, Rex and Helene, Jake and Jonquil, Bob and Constance, Steve and Mrs P, Bruce, Dave and the gang from 900 7AD, the local radio station; so many people gave hospitality. Elizabeth, your teddy bears went down with their ship. Shirley, your drawing of "Gnome Milking" for Diana perished in the same way.

So many names are lost; our friend from "Lady Daphne" who brought us such beautiful vegetables; the skipper of the "Petuna Endeavour" who gave us the freedom of his ship. Our log books were treasure chests of the friends we made. And if I forget to mention some, as for instance I left out Chris and Ian here, it is not that we think less of them but because it hurts to dwell too long on the memories.

We took the time to check over the hull very thoroughly, though apart from tightening a small area of caulking there was little to be done. Soon we were repainted and ready to return to the water. A barge was now alongside the dredger and we were invited to moor alongside that. As usual, the professionals were looking after us, saving any further embarrassments at the yacht club. Not that we need anyone else's help to embarrass us, we can do quite well on our own, as we demonstrated by threading our bowsprit through the arms of the slip cradle as we backed off. Caught between the action of the wind and the river current there was not a lot we could do as we swung sideways. By a minor miracle we backed clear without damage, but it didn't really present the image of competence which we hope for.

The people gathered on the barge to say goodbye were nearly sufficient to sink it. When we finally did get underway there was a great rushing along the river bank, with waving and photographing galore. Steve's boat intercepted us with last minute gifts and finally, when the shore had dwindled once more to a thin hazy line, the towering grey shape of "Petuna Endeavour", outward bound at speed, passed close by to make a last farewell.

The journey north to Sydney presented few problems, though a strong following wind, as we closed the south eastern corner of New South Wales, gave some exciting sailing and the East Australian Coast Current caught us once in its three knot stream and wiped out a day's progress.

We entered the well lit Sydney harbour easily at night, taking a temporary mooring in Rose Bay and going on, when it became light, to the Cruising Yacht Club of Australia's moorings in Rushcutters Bay. The moorings were crowded with yachts preparing for the classic Sydney to Hobart race; we expected that and were hoping that Bruce and Jane, who were taking part, might arrive from Adelaide before we left again.

There wasn't much room though. We were told we could stay for one night free and two more for 25 dollars. Then out. That was fair enough, but the usual anchorage area next to the club was full of temporary moorings for the yachts being moved out to make way for the race fleet. We wanted to stay a week, as Bill and Joan were in Sydney on business and it was our last chance to see them before we left Australia.

It all worked out very amicably because it took over a week to move all the boats which were being put outside, so we borrowed one of the temporary moorings for the balance of the week. Apart from the impossibility of rowing ashore when wind and tide joined forces, that was ideal. We saw Bill and Joan, toured Sydney with them, visited our friends Rob, Virginia and Rani, whom we had met in Rhodos, made new friends Lia, Masato and Hiroshi and were visited by Vicki's old friend Jane. Not a bad week, really.

We were hoping to visit friends in New Zealand for Christmas, although we had left it rather late. In fact we crossed the Tasman Sea in fine style; with far more wind than we needed, at times causing us to drag motor tyres on a long line astern, to slow us down and keep us stern on to the huge waves. Those waves were quite the largest we had ever seen, but at least they were going our way.

It was Christmas Eve when we finally sailed into Nelson harbour, in the South Island. We anchored off the yacht club and one of the members rowed out, directed us to the correct place to clear in and offered us free use of his own mooring.

There is a joke about a girl who went to New Zealand for a week's holiday. When she returned home, her friends asked her what the country was like. "I don't know" she said, "it was closed." Trying to contact our friends over the Christmas holiday we began to understand, if not exactly to appreciate, the joke. The public telephones, using old British type coin boxes with "A" and "B" buttons, only take small denomination coins. Since the cost of calls is quite horrific, the coin boxes are soon jammed full of 10 cent coins and the phone unusable as a result. The simple answer is to phone from the Post Office, but that was closed until the New Year.

Meanwhile, life was hardly dull. On Bert's mooring we were visited by David and Jenny, who live nearby, allowed us the run of their house and took us around the countryside. Also by Gordon and Chris, who collected us, showered us, fed us, helped us and gave us spares. Eventually we contacted Adrian, who lives nearby; then, as we were about to give up, our old friends Jim and Ruth, in Christchurch. The mooring which Bert had lent us was rather exposed, though very strong, so we decided to move to the pilings which the harbour board provide for visitors. The charge of 28 dollars a week was worth paying, as these moorings were in a very sheltered position where "Dorothy Ann" should be quite safe whilst we spent a week with Jim and Ruth and their children Angela and Mark. The plan had been to spend about three months in New Zealand; already we were realising that it was nowhere near enough and the longer we stayed the more time we wanted to spend there. From Nelson we planned to visit Torrent Bay, a beautiful spot in the Abel Tasman National Park, staying for a day or two in company with members of the Nelson Yacht Club. In fact we stayed at anchor there for three weeks. There are, thank goodness, no roads in the Park. All access to the beach off which we were anchored was by sea or on foot. With a beautiful country and a mild climate, the New Zealanders like to use their legs and walk the miles of easy bush trails.

Boats came and went. Gordon's "Tusk", crewed by Steve, whom we were to meet again in California; Peter's modestly named "Apostle", first met in Nelson, always crewed by a different beautiful lady. Peter and Gaye, aboard whose "Wild Goose" we explored the nearby coast; Warren and Margaret, with "H.W.Baker", who shopped for our stores on their weekly trip to Motueka, taking the children and giving us a rare and precious rest thereby. In the completely sheltered anchorage, with its curve of sandy beach, the children could swim and play in absolute safety. The days were warm, the nights cool and pleasant. It seemed to us to be as near to paradise as one could get on earth and so far we have found nothing comparable.

When we finally set sail again, it was in company with "H.W.Baker". Together, well with us lagging behind actually, we crossed Tasman Bay and anchored for a few days in Greville harbour; a huge natural harbour entered through a narrow gap in a wall of boulders. Two yachts left as we came in. From then onward we had the place to ourselves, apart from a brief glimpse of one small cruiser. There were fish which even we could catch and wild pigs ashore, which we unsuccessfully tried to trap. We tramped for hours up a stream bed, trying to find traces of the old sawmill which had been there, but the bush had covered all remains. It was a wonderfully empty place.

Next we sailed through French Pass, with an escort of dolphins leaping and swimming around us, to enter the deep fiords of the Marlborough Sounds. Warren and Margaret had to leave us shortly afterward and we planned to spend a day or so there before crossing the Cook Strait, to the North Island. Not so. We were hailed by a passing fishing boat, invited to visit, and promised a safe, deep mooring. So we came to Wakatahuri, where Dave, Kathy, Tomlin and Tom lived. I think in fact the total population was 12, when they were all at home, but the others seldom lived there. No roads. We needed booster inoculations about then, so had them done by the doctor when he called in his converted whale catcher. Once again we did not hurry away. This tiny corner, which still boasted its own boatbuilding yard and private rail slip, contained a great collection of Lister diesel engines which, scattered tastefully around the premises, ran saws, welders, generators, the slip winding gear and a host of other machinery. They also powered both the boats based there and it was good to see all that solid and reliable British engineering giving such satisfactory service.

But Peter and Gaye had invited us to stay a while at their home in Parematta, on the North Island, so eventually we crossed the Cook Strait and found our way to the Mana Cruising Club. There we received a really warm welcome, with safe mooring at no cost to ourselves. Although we were ashore at Peter and Gaye's house for much of our stay, many of the members contrived to meet us, offering every help and kindness. A few names are remembered. Brian, Bruce (the oven you got for us worked well), John (thanks for the transport), Phil and Brenda (that was a great evening at your place). We borrowed Peter's car (a friend who works nightshifts can be a very useful ally) and explored windy Wellington, where they once had to stretch ropes across the road for pedestrians to hold as they crossed on blowy days. Now the buildings which created the worst funnelling effect have been pulled down and the policemen no longer have to raise the ropes after halting the traffic.

At last we sailed out through the Cook Strait, bound for the north. Already it was late in the year, as we discovered when, after idling past Wellington and Cape Palliser, we heard forecasts of 50 knot winds in Foveaux Strait, at the bottom of South Island. "A good job we're not down there" we said happily. But as we reached Hawkes Bay, with the lights of Napier gleaming a welcome ashore, the wind began to rise and we laid a course safely out of the bay into the open sea. We sailed 120 miles before tacking back toward the land.

It was a full gale, with overcast skies making navigation an uncertain art. Our inner forestay snapped, but the bowsprit was in service and the outer forestay took the strain until we made a temporary repair. Except for the four occasions when it was broken, we normally had the bowsprit in place when going offshore. Its protruding 10ft length was a fine hazard when entering congested harbours though, and trying to turn and moor between lines of other craft; it was therefore usually run in and lashed on the foredeck in confined waters.

As the gale finally eased, a long tack back in enabled us to sight the low and sinister outline of East Cape just before dark. We scuttled thankfully around the corner into the Bay of Plenty, where we could at last alter course to bring the wind further aft, making the ride faster, drier and far more comfortable. The rest of the journey was easy enough, but for the presence of an active volcano in our path. Unlike our old friend Stromboli, this volcano simply emits a steady stream of smoke. There wasn't much moon, or at least it set rather early, on the night when we were due to pass, we hoped, the volcano. My night vision is better than Vicki's so I extended my watch and let her sleep on, as I peered into the darkness, trying to glimpse a faint silhouette against the stars. Near dawn I thought I could make it out, safely astern at some distance, but could not be sure enough to relax. Then I saw a dim red glow. "Oh, so it does give off some light" I thought. But no, it was Venus rising into view above the shoulder of the volcano, shining redly through the overcast. It was two more weary hours before I could see we were clear, hand over, and climb gratefully into bed.

Although we approached Tauranga in the light, for which we were profoundly grateful as it is a narrow and sinuous entrance, it was fully dark by the time we entered the main channel across the harbour. Tauranga harbour boasts an enormous expanse of mostly shallow water, which fills and empties with each tide. This causes tidal streams of seven knots or more in the entrance, with the result that all movements in and out, even of big vessels, must take place within about 20 minutes of slack water. Our timing was perfect as we slid past the towering cone of Mount Monganui at the entrance. Lifting and falling on the great swells which exploded in violence on the beach horribly close beside us, we worked helm and throttle to keep the leading lights in line. The good breeze which had carried us all the way to within a mile of the shore had died away; if the Yanmar missed a beat we would be dashed on the shingle and broken up at once. At last the long channel through rock and shoal was behind us and we crept in the darkness from one lighted beacon to another, in the main dredged fairway. We had entered at low water slack, so the rising tide would be helping us onward but now the water on either side of the channel was very shallow. Suddenly the lights of a ship showed ahead. She was backing into the fairway from a dock alongside and there was not going to be much space to spare.

I edged between the marker posts. Vicki looked round in alarm. "Hey, watch out" she said, "it's very shallow here you know." As she spoke we slid gently to a stop; our keel had been sliding through soft mud which had now gripped us firmly, preventing all further movement forward or astern. "Now what are you going to do?" she demanded. "What we have done for years, sailing off the Essex coast," I replied. "Put the anchor down, the kettle on, and wait for the tide. By the time we have had a cup of tea the tide will have risen and floated us off, the ships which are going will have gone and we will have the whole channel to ourselves in perfect safety."

Two ships slid by, very close, towering above us in the dark but far too deep to get any closer. We drank our tea in perfect safety, watching the night scene, until we swung gently to our anchor as the tide lifted us free once more.

Our chart was an old one which had been marked up by a friend to show the position of the Yacht Club, but we suspected that there had been more changes since his last visit. In the upper reaches of the channel the lights grew sparser and the navigation more hazardous. Moorings dotted the water; half unseen boats loomed up suddenly. Seeing an unoccupied mooring, and knowing that no more craft could enter on this tide, we picked it up for the balance of the night. The next day, as we were only making a brief stay, the Port Captain allowed us to lie alongside the ferry dock. This was a great help as the Yacht Club had indeed moved, to a new marina miles away from the edge of town, so we were saved a walk of two miles or so with all our stores. Since the Yacht Club was locked up tightly when we tried to visit it, we never knew if they would have found us a berth anyway.

Vicki applied her powers of persuasion to the local Hertz agency and a rental car was produced at substantially below the going rate. She is an expert haggler and seems to enjoy it, whereas I don't really, so I leave it to her and just enjoy the results. On this occasion the result was a trip to the volcanic region of Rotorua, which we had begun to think we could not afford.

Typical, in its way, of the minor oddities of travel, was the incident involving Noel and Freda. Whilst in Adelaide, the previous year, we had been invited to dinner by Merle and Ray, to meet sailing friends of theirs who were shortly moving to Melbourne. During the course of a hectic and convivial evening, showing slides and telling tales, the friends said "When you get to New Zealand, you must visit our friends Noel and Freda." They gave us the address and telephone number and we passed on to other topics. Now, wedged into a telephone box at the waterside in Tauranga, we had a problem. The friends had not written down their names nor, as they were about to move, their address. We could only remember two things to help explain the purpose of our call. Oh well, I could only end up looking rather silly, at the worst. I dialled. Noel answered the phone. "Oh, er, my name is Joshua Jones, but that probably won't mean anything to you," I began, hastily. "Your friend Vic, whose surname I've forgotten but whose wife's maiden name is the same as your surname, told us to call you when we got here."

I could hardly have blamed Noel if he had slammed down the phone muttering "Another nutter," under his breath. To my great relief though, he just said "Yes, I can never remember his name either, but he did write to me about you six months or so ago. I'll hop in the car and come down right away." That led to the luxury of more hot showers and a superb dinner, in their charming home overlooking the water. It is perhaps typical of the New Zealand way, of which they are so rightly proud, that Noel, a doctor of medicine, is the designer of one of New Zealand's most successful class boats. The New Zealander doesn't ask you, as I have been asked in England, "But what do you DO?" as if what one "does" is ordained and unchanging for all time; he asks "What are you doing NOW?" assuming that you can achieve whatever you set your hand and mind to. Because he will!

From Tauranga, after our visit to the steaming geysers and bubbling mud of Rotorua, we made our way cautiously up to Auckland; the most beautiful city I have seen, though parts of the centre are now being reduced by greedy and short sighted property developers to a shoddy copy of the world's other concrete jungles.

We were able to get a berth at crowded Captain Cook Wharf, right in the city centre, simply because we carry a ladder. The tidal rise in Auckland is substantial and this particular section of quay was equipped with no ladder, so no one else would moor there. With our own ladder unlashed from the rail and tied to the rigging we were not bothered that the boat was 15ft below the quay level at low water.

Alongside us, also making use of that handy ladder, was Ty, an American friend, who had just crossed from Valparaiso in 53 days, sailing alone in his Contessa

"Gigi", after his second rounding of Cape Horn. Ty also had one of the awful autolemons, identical in all respects to ours; he took this defunct helming device to the local agent. "But sir" the salesman exclaimed indignantly, "it's got WET."

"Well, yes," explained Ty patiently, "it's meant to be attached to the tiller, out in the cockpit. It gets wet there."

"Couldn't you put a plastic bag over it?" asked the salesman brightly. "Are you real?" asked Ty, hoping that the salesman was part of some Alice in Wonderland type dream. Unfortunately he, like far too many of his kind, was a part of the world we live in.

Our stay in Auckland was far too brief, although Warren, Neil, Marcia, David, Rebecca, Dennis, Paddy, Bill and Faye ashore, plus Ty, Dean, Rick and Rebecca, afloat, did their more than adequate best to make it memorable. With Dennis's van Vicki collected cases and sacks of bulk stores.

Alongside us, on neighbouring Marsden Wharf, the "Enterprise New Zealand" crew worked frantically to prepare for the Whitbread "Round the World" race. When we dropped exhausted into our bunks at night, their floodlights blazed on, as they worked around the clock.

In drenching rain they left at last; a marching band played "The Saints" and we waved through the murk. At once they were hammered by gales. Mechanical failures plagued them and though they struggled on and on, they were eventually forced to retire. Funny though; I have no idea who won the prizes, but I will always remember that, in spirit, those New Zealanders could never be beaten.

We left shortly afterward, only a few days before French saboteurs attacked the "Rainbow Warrior" in that same dock, damaging the ship and murdering a crew member, in a disgusting act of war which will have further hardened New Zealand's resolve to stamp out Nuclear tests in the Pacific.

Of course it is inevitable that the lunatic elements of

the "Greenies" make the world's headlines. Our next stop was at the little island of Waiheke, where we called on Judy, whose brother Dave had driven us all around Devonport, Tasmania, in his Mini. Judy, too, has a Mini; she also has two children and a wicked sense of humour, so she made me drive all eight of us around the island, giving her neighbours plenty of cause for speculation. From Judy we learned that many of the Greenpeace supporters come from that tiny island; sober, thinking people, with no interest in self-publicity, just a deep desire to create a better, safer world for their children. Right or wrong, there is no doubt that the French have brought Greenpeace more support with one bomb than years of campaigning could bring.

From our anchorage in the bay, below Judy's house on the hill, we sailed north to Whangarei. It is half a day's sail from Marsden Point, at the river mouth, to the town quay. We were tired by the time we arrived and rather unhappy as we saw the low bridge which blocks further progress, without finding a spot to tie up. Then a cheerful American voice called "Tie up alongside us, if you like." Tom and Dela were great fun to be with. They too were going north and left a few days later, but we were to meet them again.

Half way down the river was a tidal grid, two great upright posts with heavy timbers laid in the mud alongside them. There we tied up at high water, leaning against the posts with our keel coming to rest on the timbers as the tide fell. At low water we scrubbed off the hull and gave it a fresh coat of antifouling paint, ready for the long haul up the Pacific ocean. It cost us nothing. Our next haul out, in Hawaii, was to cost 1,000 dollars.

Back at the town quay we topped up our water tanks, cleared customs and immigration and were ready to leave. At the last moment a letter from England brought tragic news. Vicki's Aunt Marne had managed our affairs at home, forwarding mail and money, handling the sale of our house when Bob needed to move and our joint ownership was no longer practical, investing the proceeds, keeping our friends worldwide up to date with our movements and saving us much work and worry. Nearing 80 years old, she was mentally and physically vigorous, doing a part time job in addition to our chores. Now, abruptly, she had died. With heavy hearts we set sail. There was nothing to do but get on with the voyage which she had done so much to make possible. Even now, because of her forethought, we had no problem; she had insisted on having a deputy able to take her place, "In case" she would say, "I go gaga." She would not be there to welcome us home. She would not type our book, as we had promised she should. But she would never "go gaga" as she had feared and hated the thought of; we must just be glad of that, for her sake. Mike, who now took over that difficult job, half a world away and with only a brief letter or phone call every few months from which to glean our intentions and needs, rose magnificently to the occasion, though none of us imagined the complexity of the problems with which he would finally have to cope.

A squally evening as we headed down river demanded our attention. Survival leaves little room for sorrow. We groped our way into Urquhart's Bay, at the river mouth, anchored almost on top of some rocks just awash in the blackness, hastily moved on and finally found a safe spot for the night.

Overnight, the wind died, and so, on a still, misty morning in mid June, one week after my 50th birthday, we left New Zealand for the islands of the South Pacific.

11
South Seas

Our first destination was the tiny island of Aitutaki, in the Cook Islands. Theoretically it should have been an easy sail, but once again the weather had not read the books and did as it pleased. We had a bumpy, wet beat to windward; the now familiar deck leaks letting in streams of water and the rising temperature as we went north making the damp, stale air below like warm soup.

Aitutaki is not very big; about seven miles across the entire atoll, with a single hill rising to about 150 ft at one end. It is about 2,000 miles from New Zealand and there is nothing but sea, and maybe an uncharted reef or two, in between. It was a really breathtaking sight as the island rose in solitary splendour from the ocean ahead of us.

Most of the exciting photographs of Pacific islands which one sees are taken from the air; the view from the deck of a small boat being rather less spectacular as a rule. But Aitutaki is amazing from any viewpoint. The high part of the island is at one end of the atoll; the lagoon and its fringing reef, barely above water, stretching away to one side in a riot of colour almost beyond belief. We approached at an angle which enabled us to sail parallel to the reef, enthralled by the infinite shades of green and blue in the shallow waters, contrasted with the pure white spray from the endlessly breaking surf. It would be a thrilling sight from any approach, but the sensation of seeing it from a boat which we had refitted, maintained and sailed with our own hands, after four weeks spent crossing a completely empty ocean, 18,000 miles from home, was superb.

The official charts for the area, whether British, New Zealand or American, have one thing in common. They are inaccurate. The location of the island and the approaches to it were accurately known and charted, like so much of this area, by the beginning of the 20th century. The vital entrance channel through the reef, however, has been changed by blasting in recent years and we were fortunate in having on board an American publication giving a sketch of the new pass.

Our first attempt to enter was a failure. The sea constantly pours over the windward edge of the reef into the lagoon, causing a permanent outflow from the pass, which is on the leeward side of the atoll. The trade winds generally blow strongly out of the entrance also. There is a tidal action and we had timed our entrance to take advantage of the favourable stream, but at our four knot maximum speed under power we could barely move ahead. As we moved nervously forward through the churning, swirling water, we could look down on the vertical sides of the channel, at the sharp coral edges with only a few inches of water over them. The wind increased and we began to move backward; we were not going to make it and we had better get out before we got into trouble.

There was no room to turn, the pass was barely 50ft wide, far less than "Dorothy Ann", with her long keel and low power, needed for such a manoeuvre. I closed the throttle a trifle, trying to keep us pointing straight ahead as the current carried us out backward to safety. For a little while all went well, then we began to swing close to the sharp coral edge. We could not go ahead to straighten up, for we would hit the coral before we could begin to turn. If we went astern the bow would blow round even more quickly, perhaps striking the knife edged coral as it swung. But we were drifting rapidly sideways by then and in a few moments we were swirled out through the entrance, into the open sea. There was a tiny shelf, about 60ft deep, just by the mouth of the pass, where the outflowing current fought with the swells breaking on the reef at the sides to produce a maelstrom of churning water. We tried, briefly, to get an anchor to hold on this patch, but it dragged out into deep water and we decided that it was less trouble to drift for a short while, then motor back.

We had some lunch, then I adjusted the throttle cable, which I had recently repaired and which was not moving over quite its full travel. With a few more revolutions as a result of my efforts, we headed in once more and, after a few nerve wracking moments as we almost came to a halt again, we managed to push over the worst bottleneck to where the current was a little weaker. It was easy then. The pass is well marked and the little American sketch was accurate, warning of a shoal patch and indicating which side of the channel was deepest. As we neared the end, Beth, a New Zealander, rowed over to show us the best mooring spot. We dropped anchor astern of "Tern", a lovely Herreschoff designed ketch which Beth's husband Wayne had built and which they had sailed from New Zealand with their two very small children on board.

Because Aitutaki's main export is bananas there is a ban on bringing them in from elsewhere, for fear of introducing diseases or pests. The man from Agriculture quarantine came to check and spray our boat. Normal enough, but he brought with him a huge stalk of bananas to replace any which he might have to confiscate.

Later, another English couple, Shirley and Howard, came into the pass and anchored their boat "Jabberwock" astern of us. At Wayne's suggestion we all joined his family aboard "Tern", for a trip to the motus, tiny uninhabited islets, at the far side of the lagoon. "Tern" is a fairly shallow boat, fitted, as are the Thames and Dutch barges, with leeboards, which can be lowered on the outside of the hull to give good sailing performance to windward, but when raised allow "Tern" to navigate in depths of only three feet. Wayne is an expert reef navigator, having spent years exploring Australia's Great Barrier Reef, and the shallow "Tern" was built for just that type of sailing. We weaved our way between massive coral heads, through the unmarked channels into the deeper waters of the lagoon, with never a false move. Shirley, Howard and ourselves had our dinghies towing astern. We planned to spend a night aboard "Tern" then sail back next day, with the prevailing wind, leaving Wayne and Beth to stay a few more days.

It started well. We arrived safely, anchored in a good spot and set off in the dinghy to catch fish for our supper. Wayne and Howard went into the water with spear guns and I kept station on them with Wayne's dinghy. We were near where the water pours into the lagoon from the open sea, constantly changing and very cold. Soon Howard was attacked by cramp and struggled with some difficulty back into the dinghy. I was very glad I was not in the water, as I had discovered that I too am prone to cramp nowadays. Wayne, younger and tougher, was happy to go on hunting. There were few fish however and we finally ended up with just one eel-like trumpet fish; not a very large one, either. Knowing our limitations, Vicki and I had brought along a reserve of canned goods. Shirley and Howard too had the wisdom to bring chicken legs. So, with some coconuts which we gathered, we had plenty to eat around our campfire on the deserted beach. There had been some talk of sleeping ashore, but the coconut crabs scuttling on the sand, and other things rustling unseen among the trees, convinced everyone that "Tern" offered a cosier bed for the night.

Amazingly, the capacious "Tern" accommodated all 11 of us in comfort. We spent a peaceful night, breakfasted aboard and then the dinghy parties set off. In the manner of weather, the strong, steady wind, which had blown constantly since our arrival, now died away and fitful airs began to come from other directions. Shirley and Howard had a small outboard motor. They set off and drew steadily away from us. We rowed clear of the motu and attempted to set sail in the open lagoon. It was a makeshift rig; our tubby little dinghy was a good load carrier but we had no illusions about its sailing abilities. All we had expected to do was blow downwind. Now the wind settled down to blow the other way. The only option was to drop the sail and row on as best I could. It was a good five miles across to the anchorage; with the wind against me and the dinghy laden with people and bedding we were going to have a job to get there by nightfall. In the distance, Shirley and Howard could be seen landing on a small rocky island in the middle of the lagoon. A long time later, after they had gone on, we reached the island, pulled up the dinghy and stopped to rest.

When we set off again it was blowing harder against us. We were beginning to think that we would have to spend an uncomfortable night ashore in the jungle somewhere, when a sports power boat came planing across the water and stopped beside us. The customs officer (another Howard) was sitting on the foredeck. "I'm going across to tell Wayne that staying on the motus is not allowed" he said. "I'll ask him to pick you up on his way back, or you won't make it by tonight."

Later we heard that, in the recent past, another yacht had gone across the lagoon, grown cannabis on one of the motus and refused to leave, when asked to do so on the expiry of the crew's visas. Much as I dislike bureaucrats, it is hard to see what choice the authorities have but to impose more and more restrictions when faced with such stupidity and bad manners. At least in this case bad news for Wayne was good news for us, as first we, then Shirley and Howard, were picked up and taken home in comfort.

After a week in Aitutaki we set sail once more, heading for Bora-Bora in French Polynesia. There are three main groups of French islands; the Societies, the Tuamotus, further east, and the Marquesas, to the north of the Tuamotus. We were limiting our visit to the Societies, which are high islands with fantastic ragged peaks and precipitous valleys.

The Tuamotu archipelago, though the individual atolls are small, covers an area as big as New Zealand. As the islands are true atolls, only standing a few feet above sea level, they are impossible to see until very close, so it is a very dangerous area to navigate in, particularly at night. Without sophisticated navigation equipment, we thought the risks were too great for us to sail there. In fact both the Tuamotus and the Marquesas were rather far to the east of our planned route. Their principal appeal is to the yachtsman travelling west about, as they are the first islands lying across the commonly used trade wind route from Panama, over 4,000 miles away; except for the isolated Galapagos islands, which lie relatively close to Panama.

Our intention was to go north, to Christmas Island, in the Pacific ocean, just so we could say we'd been to both Christmas islands, then up to the Hawaian islands and across to San Francisco. But first we would visit Bora-Bora, Tahaa, Raiatea, Huahine, Moorea and, largest and most famous of the Society islands, Tahiti.

We saw our first low atoll, Mopelia, en route to Bora-Bora. Knowing that it was close to our path, we were very anxious to see it before nightfall. Our sights put it quite close, but we were still working to windward and sights taken from a small boat under those conditions are best regarded with a degree of caution. Vicki and I stared at the horizon until our eyes watered; not a thing could we see. Suddenly Vicki had an inspiration. Rushing below, she returned with a hand bearing compass and......Catherine. She stood on deck behind a puzzled Kate, clamped an arm around her, rested the compass on Kate's head, squinted through it and rotated her on to the bearing where Mopelia should be. "Now Kate, can you see anything?" she asked anxiously. "D'you mean all those palm trees?" asked Kate casually. "Palm trees, PALM trees?" we exclaimed in amazement. I strained my eyes, peering through the binoculars. There was a faint grey smudge, just visible where Kate was pointing.

Palm trees it was, as we eventually saw for ourselves in the last of the daylight. Now that we knew exactly where the danger lay, we could safely approach close to the downwind side of the atoll. We wanted to see just how much was visible by moonlight. It wasn't much. From two miles away, even though we knew it was there, the island was lost against the blackness of the sea. There is no permanent population; as on many atolls, there is no reliable water supply. A lamp gleamed briefly, a lone fisherman or coconut collector perhaps, then the atoll returned to blackness.

The one other hazard, Maupiti, an even smaller atoll, was safely passed close by in daylight. Bora-Bora, with its towering twin peaks, good navigation aids and plentiful shore lights, presented no problems. But in fact we were off the wide, easy pass through the reef in early afternoon. Anchorage in the Societies is often in depths of 90ft or more, something which we got used to later. Here though, we were glad to discover an unoccupied mooring outside the Oa-Oa hotel. Greg and Elaine, who run the Oa-Oa, are part of that select band of people who appear to have been placed on earth solely to be kind to yachtsmen. They provide moorings, water from their water maker, showers and the freedom of their hotel. All they ask in return is a one page entry in their visitors' log; something which most yachties delight in producing. Of course, they sell a few beers as well, but no one is made to feel under any obligation to spend; most of us are delighted to have a bar, with a dinghy dock outside, so conveniently to hand.

Ashore, Vicki was glad of the chance to speak French for the first time, apart from a few brief occasions, in years. Once fluent, she now had to think hard when she wanted to speak. Oddly, although her accent, grammar and pronunciation are vastly superior to mine, when she gets stuck for a word I can usually supply it. At least it makes me feel useful. The children had been having French lessons as part of their schooling on board. This seemed a good opportunity for them to hear the real thing and try out their own skill. Hilary set out for the local shop one day to buy a pencil sharpener, but returned without it.

"Didn't they have any?" we asked.

"I couldn't see one," came the reply.

"Did you ask?" we enquired, puzzled.

"They don't speak English," she said.

"But you speak enough French to ask for one" we exclaimed.

"Yes," came the crushing retort "but not enough to understand their answer."

A delightful French couple, Andre and Catherine, moored their yacht "Ecume" near us. They had visited the Line islands on their way south from the U.S.A. and gave us the names of friends in Fanning Island. They also recorded tapes to go with the children's French lessons, because we had been unable to afford the commercially produced ones to go with their books.

We found living rather expensive; no free bananas here and an exchange rate at the local bank far worse than we had got in New Zealand, so our cash was going much faster than we had anticipated. We needed to keep moving as we had not arranged for any more cash to be sent before we reached Hawaii. We made brief stays in Tahaa and Raiatea, two separate islands within one enclosing reef, then sailed on to Huahine. That was another near-paradise. A safe anchorage with golden sand nearby; enough boats to provide convivial company, without overcrowding, and a long passage inside the reef, with distant anchorages, to explore when we wanted a change. Many of the friends with whom we sailed and barbecued in Huahine later gave us hospitality at their homes in the U.S.A. Niels and Becky, Howard and Dana, Joe and Cathy. Andre and Catherine were there, Gary and Sabine, who journeyed safely on to Australia, Paige and Hovita, with their family, almost broke, but later to land a plum job in American Samoa. Peter, aboard "Yehudi", who lent me a cylinder head gasket when the Yanmar finally broke down. Wendy, the cheerful, helpful Belfast girl, camping on the beach, who fled from the attentions of the Tahitian boys and took refuge for a night aboard "Dorothy Ann". There were too many names to list them all, and later on there came many more. I shall continue to mention as many as I can; it would be a dull book and indeed a dull world, without people in it. One whose name I have forgotten deserves better for sure. We were seated on his stern deck, quietly drinking and chatting one evening, when I chanced to mention meeting Ross and Margaret, in London. "I was there in St Katharine's Dock too" he said. "I have just left them, in Papeete." Papeete is the capital city of the

Societies, located on Tahiti. Quickly we asked Richard, aboard "Gai Charisma" if he would use his ham radio to pass a message via his contacts in Tahiti. He did, and we arranged a meeting with "Girl Morgan" in Moorea, the island lying between Huahine and Tahiti.

We had a small mutiny on the day we left Huahine. I had been to see the gendarme, who had signed the green card used to record entry and departure to and from each island. Kate rowed ashore in the dinghy to meet me. "Daddy, can we stay another day please." "Well no, I have just got the clearance signed, ready to leave for Moorea." "I'm not going, there is a birthday party for Chris tomorrow night and all the other children are going and we never have any fun and you're horrid and I'm staying here." She leapt out of the dinghy and sat down on the beach. Poor Kate, I don't suppose anyone would have bothered if we had stayed another day, but we try to stick to the rules and we do seem to avoid a lot of problems which others complain of. However, perhaps this was a time for making an exception. There were 14 children on the boats anchored off Fare that day; often there had been no one of their age group to talk to and play with. I insisted and Kate, good soul that she is, gave in, but it really was a shame that she missed the party.

Moorea is by far the most spectacular and exciting of the Society islands, with its jagged rocky peaks rising from the sea to disappear into filmy clouds above. Weird holes pierce the rocks, luxuriant vegetation riots below. The reef encloses safe, sandy anchorage in depths of 12ft or so, where we could dive from the bowsprit into crystal clear water, quartering the bottom to search for exotic shells.

Ross and Margaret's "Girl Morgan", crossing paths with us after 3 years and over 30,000 miles sailed by the two boats since our last meeting, was still well stocked from a stay in the West Indies. Lightening the cargo by several bottles of rum did nothing to reduce the pleasure of our meeting! Jim, too was with them again, having decided that the hardships of life on board were preferable to the rigours of living in Bradford in winter.

Together we walked, swam, rowed, explored and swapped stories. When we continued on our separate ways, life seemed to lose a little of its colour.

It was necessary to go to Papeete in order to clear from French Polynesia, although we had by now realised that when people spoke of going to Tahiti they frequently meant it only to signify the islands in a general way. The bustle and uproar are fun for a day or two, but after the beauty and peace of Huahine and Moorea, Tahiti seemed sad and dusty. We spent a little time with Nick and Dorothy, aboard "Wylo II", enjoyed the company of Warren, June and Gordy, Chuck, Margaret, Ron and Annie, but after five days we were glad to go.

Once again we were heading north, past the tiny, uninhabited islands of Flint, Vostok, Malden, Caroline and Starbuck, to the world's largest atoll, Christmas Island. Once the site for British atomic tests, now the 25 mile wide atoll is part of the state of Kiribati. This whole group of islands, plus Fanning and Washington islands further to the north west, is known as the Line islands, because it sprawls across the equator. Now, together with the Phoenix islands, it is politically united with the old British administered Gilbert islands, "Kiribati" being the local pronunciation of "Gilberts", with the letters "ti" representing the sound "s". So, similarly, "Christmas" becomes "Kritimati", and the popular girl's name pronounced "Sita" is spelt "Tiita"!

All this we learned later. As we found a useful breeze, after two days of light airs north of Tahiti, we were more concerned with avoiding the unlit and uninhabited islands in our path. The currents can be strong and treacherous; normally running at up to two knots to the westward, they may abruptly reverse direction. In the empty ocean there is no way to gauge their strength or direction. Most of the islands have no drinking water and no safe landing places; hidden reefs often extend well beyond the visible areas. So careful were we to avoid the risk of being set down onto the islands by night that we never came close enough to sight any of them by day. That was a pity as, unknown to us, a yachtsman was stranded on Caroline Island at that time. By the most incredible good fortune an oceanographic survey vessel passed in sight of the island, saw his distress signals and was able to get a boat ashore to rescue him. It was the first time in three years that they had visited the island and there are few other vessels passing that way. "Caroline Island", the Admiralty Pilot says, "has no water supply."

At last we were approaching the vicinity of Christmas Island, safely past the smaller islands but concerned lest we might pass to the east of the island and be swept into the treacherous and aptly named Wreck Bay. An isolated island will usually produce a nice cumulus cloud of its own, on a clear day at sea, but that day there was a lot of cloud cover and we weren't sure which was over land. Once again it was Vicki, aptly enough, who solved the problem. "I have read that sometimes it's possible to see the green of the atoll reflected on to the clouds" she said. And there, when we knew what to look for, was a line of cloud with a dark green underbelly. Soon we could make out the now familiar grey line of the palms, as they were alternately revealed and hidden by the swell. Approaching by moonlight, we stood on and off, at a safe distance from the gleaming beach, until the pale glow of dawn gave the signal to close the land. We approached in fine style. Dolphins leapt from the water around us; the sun shone brilliantly; the island gleamed green and gold.

Close in, by the shore, was silhouetted a black hull, with spars towering above it. What could it be? A square rigged vessel here? Was it in commission or derelict? The brilliant sun threw the black hull into stark, unrevealing silhouette against the brilliant beach. Then we saw a flash of colour, a flicker of scarlet at the end of the mizen gaff. The breeze hardened, catching the cloth, and the Red Ensign unfolded and flew out bravely over the glittering blue water.

It was the British sail training vessel, "Zebu", a one time Baltic Trader, now re-rigged with square sails on the mainmast. She was taking part in "Operation Raleigh", an adventurous scheme to give a total of 4,000 young people a chance to see the world, whilst taking part in various projects for the benefit of others ashore. "Zebu"s crew of 16 boys and girls, from several nations, had been working on a project in Hawaii. Now they would sail on to New Zealand, to be replaced by another crew as they moved on to other adventures. They were lively, friendly, talented people. Catherine was soon climbing the rigging of their mainmast, hanging outward from the futtock shrouds where the mast sections join, as I had long ago told her the real sailors always did; spurning the safety of the "Lubber's hole" in the centre of the platform, against the mast.

"Zebu" was making only a short stay. We had dinner with Nick, Jane and their crew, then rowed across to "Dorothy Ann" as they prepared to get under way. The tropic night was falling swiftly, as they broke out their anchor and moved ahead of us in the dusk, looming huge against the luminous sky. Slowly they circled us, as the crews cheered each other till the echoes rang in the palm trees. Then they squared away and headed out to the south west. Much later, we received a letter from our friend Chris, in Tasmania. "Look at this wonderful boat, which came to visit Hobart," she said. "Did you ever see them in the Pacific?" And there, enclosed with her letter, was a photograph of "Zebu".

In the morning, after "Zebu" had left, we set out to enter the lagoon. We had been anchored off the open beach, which is as close in as a boat of "Zebu"s size can approach the island. The pass is not well marked and even if the chart was accurate we would have only a few inches between our keel and the sand in places. We wound our way across dark coral patches, motoring slowly and constantly sounding with the lead. Our electronic echo sounder had failed us when we needed it most, in the Gulf of Suez, and we had not bothered to fix it. A lead line is less convenient, but there isn't much to go wrong. Safely across the coral, we could see the white sand gleaming ever closer beneath us. We never seemed to actually touch, but must have come very close to doing so as the lead showed the exact depth of our keel in half a dozen places. We were unlikely to find anyone able to tow us off if we stuck there. Regrettably, the anchorage is made easy to see, by the piles of rusting junk dumped by the British forces. Just why we have this passion for destroying what we cannot take away, I have never understood. Cranes, grading machines, trucks, tons of new spare parts, all had been driven into the sea or dumped on the beach.

Probably the Kiribati folk have no interest in these things, certainly an eight cylinder Rolls-Royce diesel engine rests abandoned in its crate on the quay, but then the equipment could have been simply parked in some distant spot under the palms, rather than creating this appalling eyesore in a place of great natural beauty. There were originally two villages flanking the pass, London and Paris. Now half the island is a bird sanctuary and Paris has long been deserted. London has a customs post, store and power station (closed down at midnight).

Perry, once district officer, later plantation manager, now a Kiribati citizen, invited us to dinner on his wife, Erena's birthday. It was a joyful occasion. Joined by George and Jan from the neighbouring yacht "Io" and a few Kiribati friends, we were wined and dined in style. Later we settled down to watch a video film, rented in honour of the event. It was an epic of the American Civil War, and seemed likely to go on for a long time. Suddenly the set blacked out, as midnight came and the power station shut down for the night. The resourceful Perry had anticipated that though. Out came a Japanese portable generator, the cord was pulled and the set burst back into life. True the effect was rather marred by a pattern of white streaky lines across the screen, which effectively prevented any sight of the action, but honour was satisfied and none of us were too distressed by the prospect of being spared a further hour or two's viewing.

The Line islands are rather distant from the main islands of Kiribati and not very important in the overall scheme of things. Consequently they are seldom visited by ships and there is little communication between the islands. We were asked by several people, including the customs officer, if we would take things to Fanning Island for them. Naturally we agreed to help; it was fun and made us feel useful. Johnny, who runs a small store, asked if we could carry a few packages for him. When we agreed, he arrived on the quay with a truck full of rice, flour, soap and other goods. We didn't dare take all of it. If the weather got rough it would all get wet, and we weren't about to be held responsible for that particular little lot.

In fact our trip to Fanning Island was quite uneventful. Once again we were able to sight the island in daylight, although darkness fell before we reached it and we once again stood off at a safe distance till dawn. It was as well that we did not attempt to enter the pass at night. The entrance is narrow, the currents strong; a big swell breaks across it and once inside, coral heads abound. George and Jan had visited the island in "Io", before going to Christmas Island, so we had the benefit of their information and advice. This enabled us to pick an anchorage well clear of the tidal stream which rushed out of the pass after each high water. We once ventured too close to the entrance in our dinghy and were being swept backward out to sea, despite both rowing as hard as we could, when we had the good luck to be taken in tow by a power boat.

Here were Andre and Catherine's friends, Tabia, his wife Tapeta and the school teacher Waka. We invited them to a meal aboard "Dorothy Ann", where we discovered that they were expert gin rummy players. They then feasted us ashore, on fresh lobster and crab, raw fish (delicious), breadfruit and coconuts. Every day they brought us new gifts of fruit and vegetables. When we left we carried gifts for members of Tabia's family in Hawaii.

There was a solitary British citizen on Fanning Island, Alan, who ran the local store. The store had belonged to the company which used to work the plantations; Alan had taken it over when, after independence, the Kiribati government took over the plantations themselves. Now he was being put under pressure by the local politicians. The rent for the store had been raised tenfold and he had received a demand to pay the extra amount for the previous three years also. Clearly the intention was to make it impossible for him to stay; at the same time robbing him of all reward for his years of work on the island. He was quietly preparing his own boat, ready to abandon his home and business if the situation worsened.

After a week on the island, we said goodbye to our friends, reflecting once again on the fact that politicians and people are two very different things. Attempting a stylish departure we started the motor, raised all sail and smartly broke out the anchor. We promptly touched on an isolated coral head, came to a dead stop and began to swing round helplessly, under the pressure of the strong trade wind funnelling down the lagoon. Worried that we might break free facing shoreward, promptly running further aground in the shallows, I let go the anchor again. As I did so, Vicki, at the tiller, shouted "We're free" and we slid off the coral. I frantically dragged in chain, fearing that the anchor would bite, or snag another block of coral, stopping us once again before we could reach safer waters. We were lucky. I got the anchor back on deck without further incident, as Vicki motor-sailed us out to the centre of the pass. Once in the main outgoing stream we were swept rapidly out to sea; much to our relief, for to touch bottom in the pass would probably mean disaster as the swells broke up the boat. Once clear of the island, we set course for Hawaii.

We were prepared for a difficult journey. The Hawaian, or Sandwich Islands, as the chart calls them, are a chain of seven inhabited and numerous uninhabited islands. The "Big Island" of Hawaii is in about 20 degrees north latitude; the rest of the chain stretching away in a north westerly direction to about 30 degrees north. Mention the name Hawaii and most of us probably think of Honolulu, Waikiki Beach and perhaps Pearl Harbor. These however are in fact all on the relatively small island of Oahu, in the centre of the chain. It is of course the business created by the proximity of the Naval base which has caused the development of Honolulu. The vast, natural harbour was an obvious choice of base for the U.S. Pacific fleet.

Because the islands sit squarely in the path of the trade winds, which blow strongly from the north east, it is difficult to sail through them in an easterly direction. Our intention was to enter at Hilo, on the north east tip of the Big Island, then work our way westward. The essential thing was to work our way well to the eastward after leaving Fanning Island, before we went far enough north to feel the effect of the trades.

At one time we had intended to visit Palmyra, to the west of Fanning, where Andre and Catherine had spent some time on their journey south. Although U.S. territory, it is now totally deserted except for passing yachts and the occasional visit by a U.S. coastguard vessel. There is safe anchorage in the lagoon, good water and the reef teems with fish. There is even a bathtub, out in the open, which is heated by lighting a fire under it. It was a long way to the west though, and time was passing. If we intended to cross the North Pacific that year, we needed to press on rapidly. Reluctantly we decided that we must head east, using the Equatorial Counter Current and the variable winds of those latitudes, whilst we could.

For the next few days we plodded along through showers, calms and sudden squalls. Then, to our delight, a steady breeze from the southeast enabled us to sail a northeasterly course with ease. Our usually unrewarded efforts at fishing suddenly resulted in almost embarrassing success.Fish had previously disregarded the most tempting baits, even though they were leaping from the water all around us. Now they snatched ravenously at any old bit of white plastic on a hook. We caught several with the base of a discarded plastic cigarette lighter as bait. We would put the lines out, pull in two or three fish, all that we could eat in a day, then wind up the lines to avoid catching more.

This idyllic existence continued all the way to Hawaii. We easily worked out to 150 degrees west longitude, as recommended in the old sailing directions given in "Ocean Passages for the World", then headed due north. The weather broke as we sighted the island; the last night was a constant battle, with thunder and lightning, savage squalls thrashing the sea into waves then leaving us windless and wallowing in a chaos of thrashing spars and blocks.

The violent motion created by a rough sea with no wind to give direction to the waves and steady the ship, is the most damaging condition for a small boat at sea. The lashing holding the mainsheet block to the boom, many turns of hefty synthetic rope, was snapped like wet string, allowing the mainsail to thrash about wildly until it could be brought under control. Standing on deck was impossible; even when sitting it was necessary to hold on, to avoid being thrown around. Any work had to be done one handed, which made for slow progress. Running backstays were jerked out of their cleats, foresails thrashed from side to side, tangling their sheets. When wind came, briefly, it was always from a different direction. No sooner would we trim the sails than they would be aback, forcing us to slacken sheets just tightened and trim the opposite ones again.

At last the sky paled into the new day. The clouds fled, the sun rose, gleaming on a wreath of snow and the twin towers of the observatory, high on the slopes of the 13,000ft volcano Mauna Loa. We motored across calm and placid water into Hilo Harbor, crossing its full length to Radio Bay, where the transient yachts moor. Dan, whom we had first met aboard his yacht "Illusions" in Huahine, rowed over and took our lines ashore, as we anchored with our stern toward the quay.

12
Polynesia U.S.A.

Our arrival date was November 28th, Thanksgiving Day, which is of course a public holiday in the U.S.A. So, the Hawaian islands being the 50th State of the Union, we were running true to form. We would have to pay a hefty overtime fee if we wanted to clear customs and immigration that day, so, in the interest of economy, we resigned ourselves to a further day aboard without fresh bread or milk.

Then the customs officer phoned the port office with a stern message. "If they aren't clearing in until tomorrow, no one but the skipper can go into the town for stores." I was off down the road in a flash. We even had a few U.S. dollars held in reserve, so no matter that the banks were closed. Most of the businesses and small shops were closed too, but there on the outskirts of town was that wonderful American aid to the would-be adventurer, the Supermarket. Not the pale imitation which we have in Britain, but the genuine article, bursting with every imaginable thing to eat, including shelf after shelf of lovely fresh vegetables and fruit.

There really is nothing like spending a few months living mostly on canned and dried foods to increase one's appreciation of, say, cabbage and potatoes. Although grown in some of the high islands of the tropics, most vegetables are scarce, expensive and often of dubious quality in the places which we had recently visited. Few things, apart from potatoes and onions, will keep on board for more than a day or two, even where they are available. Hawaii, though, has it all. The tremendously fertile volcanic soil, the climate tempered by the trade winds, and the high altitudes, enable any imaginable thing to be grown in quantity. The Parker Ranch, largest in the U.S.A. is located on Hawaii Island. Juicy papayas, breadfruit, grow like blackberries in England. Great, buttery, soft avocado pears grow prolifically, on huge trees bearing 2,000 pounds of the fruit at one time. I staggered back to the boat with two huge bags of fresh food and we were quite happy to eat, drink and laze around until Mr Moore came down to clear us, swiftly and efficiently, the next day.

Shortly afterward, Cathy and Joe, who had scuba dived to free our anchor when we snagged it in 90ft of water at Huahine, sailed in aboard "Viajero". Later we also met Ann and Andy, who had sailed an old, converted, ship's lifeboat down from Portland, Oregon; taking seven weeks to reach Hilo. Unable to afford a liferaft, they had fitted a buoyancy system to "Integrity", so that she would not sink even if holed below the waterline. It consisted of a number of large truck inner tubes, with a gas inflation system. Unfortunately they could only afford one gas bottle too, so, when the system was accidentally triggered, just out of Portland, they dared not deflate it again. They were left with only a tiny area near the stern in which to sleep. Neither Ann nor Andy could be called small, so how they managed to live and remain sane in the few feet of space left to them, no one could imagine. Yet they had arrived, friendly, helpful and relaxed; apparently none the worse for the experience. Their tiller had broken too, but they used ropes attached to a hole in the rudder blade, prudently provided for emergency use, to continue to steer their craft.

Ann had bought an old car but could not afford fuel. We could afford fuel but not car rentals. We joined forces therefore, to drive and walk high on the volcano; travelling through the neglected cane fields, where much marijuana is grown in the middle of the screening vegetation, across the glittering, cooled lava slopes and down again to the black sand beaches and rolling surf.

The sugar refineries, producers of the island's main export commodity, were running at reduced capacity as market prices dropped elsewhere. In the port, warehouses and conveyors stood idle; bags of sugar still lying waiting to be loaded onto transport. Ships of the Matson line continued to bring large volumes of containers, filled with consumer goods from the mainland into the port, but nothing went out. The collapse of the sugar market and reduced military spending have affected the basic economy of the islands. As in too many places, tourism is seen as the answer, resulting in squalid commercialisation of what were once spontaneous forms of behaviour. Hawaii has remained remarkably unspoiled by this so far, but there are signs of discontent. Not all the local population, of whatever ancestry, wish to become merely caretakers of a holiday plot for rich Americans from the mainland. There isn't much of the simple life left in "Polynesia, U.S.A.", as the travel brochures style it.

One day an Australian registered boat came into the bay. Idly looking across at the newcomers we were astounded to see Marcus, whom we had last seen skippering "Unlikely VII" in Sri Lanka, with his girl friend Cindee as crew. He was skippering a delivery to the Philippines and had put in to examine a suspect rudder shaft bearing. We were delighted to hear that he and Cindee had married since we last saw them and now had a baby. Cindee would have been happy to crew, bringing her baby along, but the owners didn't like the idea so she had to stay behind, no doubt in a fine old temper.

On board, they had the "Lord of the Rings", recorded on about a dozen cassettes. Catherine borrowed them and we heard nothing else but the doings of Bilbo Baggins, Gandalf, Thorin Oakenshield and the rest for several days. The other great amusement which the children enjoyed was sailing the dinghy, with a squaresail improvised from scrap canvas, across the bay.

Due to the immense traffic of yachts, from the west coast of the U.S.A. mainly, and the shortage of good harbours in the Hawaiian Islands, visitors are allowed a maximum stay of 30 days in each harbour, during each year. That is if room is available. In some places there is no room at all for transient mooring. Radio Bay is spacious and well protected, but soon after our arrival there was a storm of sufficiently great force to drive water high over the sea wall in great foaming cascades. The harbourmaster told us that the wall had been breached by the sea on three previous occasions; even with it intact, the water pouring over caused an immense surge in the bay, making the boats rush backward to almost collide with the quay, before surging 20 feet or so back toward their anchors.

We were to learn more about Hawaian harbours later. We stayed our 30 days in Hilo, then set off intending to make a brief stop off the Kona coast, on the west side of the island, then travel quite rapidly to Honolulu where we would clear outward and go north, then east, to California. We set out in calm conditions, but after 24 hours a gentle breeze came, giving us a quiet and pleasant three day sail to our next planned stop.

Anchored in Kealakekua Bay, where Captain Cook was killed on his way south after surveying and mapping the Alaskan coast, we planned to sail next day to nearby Kailua, to buy our Christmas provisions. First however, we were going ashore to call on a lady whom we had never met, but whose sailing exploits are legendary.

It was rather later than we intended when we found the house; still, there was time for a brief call, we thought. Nancy invited us in; offered drinks. We sat and talked awhile. "Oh, so you are the people who have just come from Fanning Island," she said. "John, from the chandlery, told me about you, when he drove over to collect the gifts which you brought from Tabia". Although we knew about Nancy's voyages in the Antarctic, her three circumnavigations and over 200,000 miles of sailing, we did not realise that she has strong connections with the Line islands. In fact she is a regular visitor there, with her 58ft iron hulled yacht "Goodewind". Her partner, Terry, had just taken the yacht down to Christmas Island with a party of charterers and Nancy would be flying down shortly with another group, to sail "Goodewind" back to Hawaii.

"Help yourselves to the shower while I get dinner on;

you'll stay for a meal, of course," said Nancy. We thanked her and hastened to enjoy the luxury of plentiful hot water. The port showers in Hilo had consisted of a windowless concrete building equipped with a pipe which released a solid half-inch column of cold water, without the refinement of a shower rose. Even in the tropics it was of doubtful attraction.

"It's far too late to go out to your boat now" said Nancy as we sat talking after a magnificent dinner. "There's plenty of room here for everyone and surely you'll stay for Christmas?" "Er, well, um, are you sure?" we asked, feeling rather overwhelmed. "It will be a lot more fun with a house full of people, than just me and the children," she replied. So we stayed. And stayed. And stayed. First there was Christmas of course, which was a rousing success. Then Kate's birthday, for which Nancy made out a ticket inviting her to return to Christmas Island and help to sail "Goodewind" home. Nancy's daughter Fiona was going also and they would enjoy each other's company. Both were competent crew.

Hauling out time was upon us again, so we arranged to be lifted out at nearby Honokohau. "Good," said Nancy, "you can live in my house with my son Rob, whilst we are away on "Goodewind". You can take my car to drive over and work on the boat during the day." Everyone was advising us not to venture further north until the spring so, without any great reluctance, we settled down for a long stay. In the yard next to us was "Barefoot", a crack racing machine whose owner, Jim, had won countless events in her when he sailed out of Seattle. Now settled in Hawaii, he liked to invite us to his home to eat, talk and listen to jazz records.

Honokohau Harbor was solidly packed with boats, so we needed a new home for "Dorothy Ann" when her refit was complete. A borrowed mooring in Hawaii's only other harbour of any size, Kawaihai, solved that problem. "Goodewind" was back by then, so we invited Fiona to share a watch on the trip.

We had attempted to slink out of the house on Nancy's return, feeling that we surely would otherwise outstay our welcome. "What are you doing?" thundered Nancy. Nervously we explained that we didn't want to abuse her hospitality. "I am quite capable of telling you if I want you to go," she retorted. Hastily, we settled in again. It was no hardship to remain.

The crew of "Goodewind" had come back to the house to celebrate their triumphant return. So we met Catherine's new friends Karen and Sue, and were invited to visit them in the Yukon territory and Washington state. Bill, another member of the crew, entertained us at his home near Kawaihai. We also met Fred, Nancy's much-travelled other partner, who was to reappear again in our travels. Other yachts sailed into Kealakekua Bay, their crews treading the well known route to Nancy's door. "Skye II" with John, Kottie and their two boys, Toby and Dean, brought news from Fanning Island. Nancy, learning from us of Alan's plight, had taken him a new almanac, so that he could navigate safely if forced to flee. His boat was almost ready when his passport was confiscated and he was placed under house arrest. John had quietly finished stowing the boat and sneaked Alan aboard at night. Many months later, we heard of his safe arrival in Fiji.

Tall Nicola and short Ferdie, squabbling happily in their 24ft folkboat, "Brandywine", also came to visit. Vicki and Nancy sailed with them in the bay and we all enjoyed an afternoon spent sailing Nancy's other boat "Nelly Bly" off Honokohau. Thursday evening was "Dollar Night" at the local cinema in Kailua. Sometimes we would form a great straggling mob and pay our dollar apiece to see the latest offering, supping afterward on pizzas and beer. One evening, when Nancy was returning from a business trip to Honolulu, I arrived at the airport to collect her, with nine people already in her car. It was a confused, crowded, relaxed, happy time.

Vern and Arlene, cruising sailors temporarily ashore, also plied us with food and wine. Dan, Thea, Kurt, David, Craig, Carl, Suzy, the list of those whose friendship we enjoyed becomes endless. When at last we left, we gave a farewell barbecue at Spenser Park, near the harbour at Kawaihai. We stopped counting after the 70th guest arrived. In the end, when the party was over, Jim and Tina drove us down to the dinghy dock and produced a final bottle of "bubbly". A few last flash photos as we toasted each other, then they drove away and we rowed out, in the darkness, to "Dorothy Ann".

Although Hilo, at the windward end of the island, receives a high level of rainfall, the Kona coast, shielded by the towering heights of the twin volcanoes, Mauna Loa and Mauna Kea, has almost none. Even the rare but violent "Kona" storms, from the south, bring little rain. So once again "Dorothy Ann"s deck seams had been baked dry, despite frequent sluicings from a bucket whenever we were on board. The channels between the islands funnel the trade winds through at greatly magnified speeds, creating rough water as well. Soon we were taking heavy spray over the decks and our newly washed and dried bedding was damp again. The Alenuihaha channel, between Hawaii and neighbouring Maui, is 30 miles wide; so we could expect at least six hours of those conditions. After five months of easy living, we didn't much enjoy it.

We had hoped to visit Molokini, a tiny island in the Alakeiki channel, between Maui and Kahoolawe, formed by the rim of a volcanic crater, which the sea has breached to make a crescent of rock around a deep bay. It is said to offer magnificent snorkelling and diving, but the holding is poor and it would be a dangerous place to be caught in strong winds. However, the wind continued to blow hard, even after we reached the lee of Maui, so we anchored for the night in La Perousse Bay, on its southern tip. Because of the height of the islands, the winds are channelled with remarkable precision; it is possible to pass from a flat calm to 20 knot winds in a matter of a few yards. We spent a day at anchor. The children were able to take their rubber dinghies ashore in safety and play on the beach; but outside the bay the wind continued unabated, so that our visit to Molokini was still not possible.

We gave up and sailed to the old whaling port of

Lahaina, also on Maui. On the way, we put into the harbour of Maalea for a night, as conditions were still quite bad. The harbour was very congested and at first the harbourmaster refused to let us stay. After some persuasion though, he relented and allowed us to anchor for the night, in a spot too close to a coral reef for comfort. The harbour at Lahaina is even smaller, but anchorage just outside is quite comfortable, even though it is disconcerting to see the wind blowing quite hard just a little way away. One quiet afternoon we were watching the "whale watching" boats set out and thought we would tag along. We raised the anchor, motored off in a flat calm, raised sail just to steady the boat, which was rolling in a short, choppy sea, and were promptly knocked flat on our ear by a solid blast of wind. We had crossed the "wind line" into the area not shielded by the island, and from then on we pounded and splashed until we decided that it wasn't at all what we wanted to do and put about to return. We crashed and banged our way back to the anchorage, crossed the wind line again and suddenly found ourselves in calm and peace once more.

We stayed at anchor only a few days, then left to sail past Lanai and Molokai, crossing the Kaiwi channel to Oahu. On the afternoon of our leaving, the wind had fallen light, so we tacked slowly across toward Lanai, idly watching the whale watching boats as they cruised up and down, trying to give the charterers a sight of the humpback whales for which the area is famous. After a while we saw the great plume of spray of a whale blowing nearby. The wind freshened a bit and we altered course a little toward the whale's position. There were several more puffs of spray and we soon realised it was a group of three or more. We altered course again, to avoid going too close and disturbing them, but soon they decided to come and play with us. All the sea creatures, even the tiniest fish, can easily overtake a slow boat like "Dorothy Ann" if they wish. The humpback whales needed the merest flick of their mighty tails to keep station on us. They passed close beside us, crossed ahead, followed astern, dived underneath. One swam directly below us, visible ahead, astern and on both sides; it looked like a great platform on which we were being carried along.

Lovely, gentle, friendly creatures; they meant no harm and indeed caused no fear, despite their great size and strength. Their actions showed no trace of menace. The precision of their movement was such that, no matter how closely or rapidly they approached, they never so much as brushed against us. During the course of that afternoon and evening, no less than three separate groups of the great creatures came to play around us. We were immensely tickled to see the noisy, powered vessels of the professional whale watchers burning fuel, as they rushed fruitlessly toward one distant blow after another, only to find that the whales had sounded and sped away to another spot.

The weather was kind to us that night, as we ventured out into the exposed waters of the Kaiwi channel. Remaining light until we were far enough across to bring it well abeam, the wind strengthened nicely to bring us off Honolulu by mid morning. We found the well marked entrance to the Ala Wai Yacht Harbor, in front of the soaring skyscrapers of Waikiki beach, and were lucky enough to find an empty space among the transit moorings.

Nearby was "Viajero", with Joe on hand once more to take our lines and make us fast. Ferdie and Nicola were there too. Becky and Niels brought their huge trimaran "Alas" from nearby Keehi lagoon, squeezing up the narrow channel to our mooring to shout greetings across to us. Tom and Dela, last seen in Auckland, came to visit. Fred appeared and we took a bus ride around the island together, stopping off to swim in the surf of Waimea Bay, on the northern shore where the trades blow unobstructed, creating the famous surf of nearby Sunset Beach. Cathy drove us, in the small hours, to Diamond Head, to see a perfect view of Halley's Comet.

There were new friends here too. Polly, Harlow and David, aboard Harlow's "Ascoy", Bill and Kathy aboard "Silver Heels". At Bill's birthday party, one of his Hawaiian friends reduced us all to tears of laughter by pointing to a pasty youth in swimming trunks, obviously newly arrived on the beach, and crying "Look, look, a White Man". Yes even we, although fair skinned and prone to burn, had darkened quite a lot in our long spell under tropical skies. Enough that our new friend took it for granted that we would share his joke, which we did heartily.

Sometimes, in the middle of the day, we would need to put on flip-flops to avoid burning our feet, if walking on paved surfaces; otherwise we went barefoot, with minimal clothing. As evening came, a great fleet of apparent sailing craft would put to sea from Honolulu Harbor. These were in reality floating restaurants, with powerful engines, setting sails to give "atmosphere" only. In their solemn parade, up and down the same short stretch of the coastline, they seemed to me to resemble the ladies of a "red light" district, patrolling their pitches. We dubbed it the "Parade of the Tarts."

A month passed quickly. We topped up our stores; David's mother had a flat in Honolulu and helped Vicki to bottle jars of meat in her kitchen, for our next spell at sea. We caught the bus to Pearl Harbor, where we visited the memorial to those killed in the attack in 1942; there we bought one of the flags flown from the staff on the sunken battleship "Arizona", which is spanned by the memorial arch. It seemed appropriate to use as "Dorothy Ann"'s courtesy flag whilst in U.S. waters.

During our long stay in Hawaii we had learned to drive on the "wrong" side of the road, covering many miles in Nancy's cars. Hitch hiking is common there, as there is virtually no bus service, and we met many visitors to the island by giving them lifts. A fair number of people who had wisely come south to escape the Alaskan winter exhorted us not to miss the chance of visiting their state in the summer. Finally, a friend who had been sailing in those waters lent us charts and pilots for the Alaskan coast. Due to the need to sail north of the high pressure zone in the North Pacific before being able to head east, there is little difference in distance between sailing from Honolulu to San Francisco or to Sitka, in Alaska. So we had decided to head for Sitka, then travel up the "inside passage" between the coast and the adjacent island chain, to Skagway.

From Skagway, start of the famous Klondyke goldfields trail of the 1890s, we would travel overland to visit Karen, who had sailed in "Goodewind" with Kate, at Tagish, in the Yukon territory. On our return we would visit Glacier Bay, then start our journey south to Panama.

All too quickly it was time to go. Nicola rose early to make leis of plumeria flowers for us; tradition has it that if you throw your lei overboard to float behind you as you leave, you will return one day to the islands. We hope that it will come true for us one day. A group of friends gathered to say goodbye, we slipped swiftly out of the Ala Wai and soon were leaving our drifting leis far behind.

13
Icebergs and Expo '86

It was the first day of May, as we cleared the northern shores of Oahu in the early morning. The trades were blowing strongly, with the usual effect. Several more seams had opened up in the deck, letting water stream in large quantities straight into our bunks. Once we were clear of the funnelling effect of the Kaui channel however, the sea state was more regular and we took less water over us. A lessening of the wind for a few days gave us time to recaulk the worst offenders, with reasonable success. Just as well; we were going to feel the cold enough without being wet through as well.

For some time, as we made good progress northward, I resisted the temptation to put on footwear, thinking that it was not really cold, just a matter of adjusting to leaving the tropics. When my feet suddenly swelled up and began to itch furiously, with a fine crop of chilblains, I saw sense and put my socks and boots on.

Two shipping tracks crossed our path. A solitary ship was sighted as we crossed the route to the Philippines, three more, in two days, on the Yokohama route. They were the only signs of life outside "Dorothy Ann" during our 30 day passage.

The third week brought fog, but good wind also, so that we scudded along in a blind world. By the time we broke clear of it we should have got westerly winds, but that year there were none, as we later learned from others. Still, we managed to make fair progress, until at last we saw the glittering, snowcapped peaks of the Alaskan coast, rising out of the ocean before us. One really blinding white mass, to the north of us, puzzled us completely. If it were Mount Edgcumbe, and there was really nothing else in that direction, our sights were a good 40 miles in error. In any case, the wind was now directly offshore, so we could only beat slowly up and down the coast, making little headway toward it. Eventually, when the supposed Mount Edgcumbe seemed no closer, we got out the small scale charts, covering a much greater area. There was the answer; what we were seeing was the tip of the mighty Fairweather range, over 100 miles away.

Off Hawaii it had frequently been impossible to see the island, rising over 13,000ft above the sea, from three miles away, due to atmospheric haze. We had realised that the clear northern air would hold some surprises for us, but visibilities of over 100 miles were hard to believe.

The next day, we had a more favourable breeze; being able to reach Sitka Sound by nightfall, then motoring in calm conditions through the well lit maze of islands which lie off the town, to drop anchor; cautiously sounding our way in, until we reached a moderate depth. It took a little time in the dark and we were tempted to simply anchor near the main channel. We were glad the next day that we had worked well inshore; there was a large cruise liner anchored outside us, and it was comforting to know that she could not possibly swing into the shallows where we were.

In the morning we motored easily under the high bridge, past the packed fishing boat harbours and the floatplane sheds, to Thomsen Harbor, where we hoped to find a space. In fact not only did we find a comfortable mooring alongside, we also found the friendliest, most welcoming community you could imagine.

That first evening, over a dozen people crammed into "Dorothy Ann"s tiny saloon, talking and laughing until late at night. Among those, I must mention Dave, Everest and Clint, for they were the first to speak to us. Then Karen (not Kate's friend from the Yukon) because she was the one who arranged the dinner and slide show next evening, at which we met another 30 people.

Among those, Diane, Dennis and Maalea gave hospitality during our stay. Other members of the harbour community wined and dined us aboard their boats; Paul and Thelma, Susie, the list, as usual, becomes endless. Allen wrote our story for the "Sitka Sentinel", his wife Dawn, with memories of a holiday visit to the U.K. produced an English style meal in our honour.

Catherine was delighted to have a friend of her own age, in Clint's daughter Marivell. Moreover, Marivell had a car, which was great fun for her, even though the size of Baranof Island, on which Sitka stands, restricts the total road system to a length of a few miles.

After a chilly first week, the weather became fine and sunny for most of our stay. Those who were more acclimatised soon appeared shirtless and in shorts. We had not progressed that far in adjusting to a change of over 30 degrees of latitude, a matter of 2,000 miles or so to the north of Hawaii, but were quite warm enough in normal clothing.

It was interesting to discover how many of our neighbours were settlers from other states, still pursuing the great American tradition of seeking freedom in wild, untamed country. Dennis and Maalea had made the abrupt transition from Phoenix, Arizona, in the heat of the western deserts. Clint had ventured north from Washington state, where his wife, Janet, continued to teach until the holidays left her free to join him.

All around us people were readying fishing boats of all imaginable types and sizes, to try their luck in the harsh grounds of the North Pacific. Despite strict regulation to prevent over fishing, there are good livings to be made by the skilful and determined; by people who want to see results related to their efforts, without time clocks, strikes, or the other trappings of industrial life.

Once more a planned stay of a few days lengthened into a month. With some reluctance we finally prepared to depart. Kim and Millette, who had taught us to fillet halibut, providing both the fish and the means to cook it afterward, were determined to give us a good send off. The passage between the islands is narrow in places, with strong tidal streams. With our small motor and the wind screened by the surrounding mountains, we had to time our passages very carefully. The channels are deep, so anchorage can be difficult. With the short nights we could have gone on through the 24 hours, working watch and watch, but it would have spoiled the enjoyment of the surroundings to be helming and navigating alone, also missing the sight of half that spectacular scenery whilst asleep. So we planned to sail only by day, which meant a five a.m. start from Sitka. Not only were Kim and Millette up and about for this; they had made coffee and cooked bacon and sausages, to give us a good breakfast to start the day.

Executing our tightest possible turn, we just managed to squeeze past the fishing boats ranged along the outer breakwater and emerge into the channel. With the blue smoke haze of the Yanmar's exhaust trailing behind us in the still air, we set off for Skagway, once the gateway to the fabled Klondyke, scene of the last great gold rush.

One night we spent tied to a log boom, another at the harbour of tiny Tennakee Springs, where we bathed in the town bath house, a building over a natural cleft in the rock from which water bubbles constantly at a perfect temperature for bathing. It was an eerie sensation to realise that the cleft between our feet, as we leaned against the sloping V formed by the sides, connected eventually with the earth's heated core.

A further night was spent at anchor, uneasily, in a shallow notch in the side of the Lynn Canal, a broad, straight channel which stretches northward, an unbroken 150 miles, to Skagway. We then received wind in abundance, funnelled through the glacier capped mountains of Juneau, past Haines, terminus of the only road from Anchorage and Fairbanks, driving us onward down the narrowing way that the gold prospectors of 1898 had followed in their thousands. It was fortunate indeed that the capacious small boat harbour at Skagway was almost empty. After passing close alongside the P and O cruise liner "Island Princess", to let them see that we, too, were flying the Red Ensign, we entered the harbour and, once again, needed full power astern to avoid being blown clean out of the other side of it.

After much frantic manoeuvring we managed to get

Vicki ashore with a line, after which it was a simple matter to work "Dorothy Ann" into a berth and tie up safely. Soon we were ashore enjoying the sights of the town which "Soapy" Smith and his gang terrorised, until Frank Reid killed "Soapy" in a gun battle which cost both their lives. Much of the town has been preserved or restored, to give a flavour of those far off days, though nowadays a hard surfaced road, leading north to join the Alaska highway, has replaced the mud, ruts and plank sidewalks of the gold rush period.

Karen came down from Tagish, with her friends Rob and Mary Ann, who later drove us up through British Columbia and into the Yukon. But before that, we had met Dennis, Nancy, and their family.

Usually there were visits by one or more cruise ships every day, but for some reason one day there was a gap in the schedule which allowed Dennis, normally busy in his Alaskan ivory and Esquimo artifacts store, to take a little time off. Visiting the harbour, with son Jim, he came to chat to us, inviting us to join his family for a picnic on the beach. In time we learned that he had started his business, now worth a fortune, by dog sledding through the Arctic, trading with the Esquimaux. Along with tools, outboard motors and other items for trade, he carried domestic appliances to those distant regions. He is, in fact, the only man we have ever met who has sold refrigerators to Esquimaux.

Rob and Mary Ann were land bound sailors, running their business in Whitehorse to raise the capital for further sailing adventures. It was our good fortune that the business which they were running was a home for children in need of care. They were able to give us a ride to the Yukon in their minibus on their return from a children's outing to Skagway. Thanks to Rob and Mary Ann we saw much more of the Yukon than we could have done otherwise. Karen had arranged for us to have the use of a log cabin beside her house, on the banks of the Tagish lake. There we looked out over scenery so breathtaking that we would wake at night after only an hour or two of sleep and simply gaze enraptured at the scene outside our windows. Since it never really grew dark in those latitudes we were permanently tired, from greedily trying to see everything around us almost 24 hours a day.

One day we walked down the tracks of the disused Yukon and White Pass railway, toward the shores of Lake Bennett, where the prospectors of old had camped and built their boats. Even without packs to carry and with the smooth grade of the railway to follow, it was a hard, dusty trek. Hikers from the start of the route, at Skagway, came up the trail with little breath left; yet the prospectors each made a dozen or more trips both ways, in all weathers, to carry up the ton of supplies, which they had to bring before Canadian customs would allow them to enter the Yukon Territory.

Our schedule was getting fairly tight now, if we were to get through Panama and up to New Orleans before the start of the hurricane season in 1987, having visited all the places and people we wanted to see on the way. Hastening back to Skagway, we spent a last evening with Dennis, Nancy and their family. Dennis had come to the boat to inlay ivory eyes into the face carved on our tiller end. This he did, by the light of a pressure lamp in the cockpit, as we drank beer, crowded together, trying to do all the talking for which we had too little time.

South then to Juneau, where Kenwyn, whom we had also met walking on the quayside in Skagway, had invited us to visit his home. We stayed a short while there, driving squeezed into their huge open Buick with Kenwyn, his wife Sandra, and their three children, sightseeing, collecting stores and going on a fishing expedition. There also, we met Geoff, who told us of the Port Townsend Wooden Boat Festival, and John, who taught us to remove the shells from the great crabs, 10 inches or more across the shell, which are caught in those waters. It really is quite simple, once you have grasped the five legs on each side of the live crab firmly in your hands!

Though we sailed from Juneau in bright midsummer sunshine, there was dense fog rolling past Gustavus, on the edge of the entrance to Glacier Bay, as we approached two days later. A big problem in windless fog is that, with the sense of sight already useless, the noise of the motor destroys the sense of hearing also. So we crept very slowly into the bay, edging gingerly in until the ghostly outline of trees on the bank were visible, then cautiously keeping on a course parallel with them until we reached Bartlett Cove, where the mists thinned to allow us to see the landing stage and ranger station.

To protect the environment, entry to the bay is restricted, but we had our permits arranged in advance, so this was no problem. We went ashore to visit the lodge and take advantage of the excellent information service which the park ranger service always provides. Deciding to take a guided walk in the morning, we found ourselves lucky enough to be the only people wanting to go. So we had Kris, the ranger, all to ourselves. She took us to a squelchy patch near the bay, where we took off our shoes and paddled through the icy tussocks to a group of big boulders. There, we were able to lie in the hot sun, like lizards, on the rocks, as Kris pointed out the wildlife nearby. Later she gave us lunch at her trailer and we made a date to meet at Yosemite, where she would be in the winter season.

We spent a week exploring the bay, together with Frank and Carol, a Canadian couple sailing their yacht "Halcyone". Together we pushed through the loose ice, watching the scene of violence as huge masses split from the faces of the glaciers with the noise of thunder, pounding the still waters below into clouds of spray. There were the humpback whales again, for they cruise the length of the North Pacific to spend their summers here. Eagles soared overhead, not uncommon in the north but even more impressive in this majestic amphitheatre. On our last evening, black bear cubs were gambolling along the beach beside our anchorage.

That evening also we met Charlie and Mandy, aboard "Bastante", who had followed in our wake all the way from Honolulu. In every port they heard "Oh, do you know the Jones family? They only left a few days ago."

Their greeting to us was "So you're the famous Joneses." Which is how Frank and Carol now address their letters to us.

A brief, one night visit to tiny, jewel like, Elfin Cove, for some fresh provisions, and we sailed outside the islands once more to begin our journey south. With the lack of wind in the channels, or worse, the chance of headwinds, together with the Yanmar's growing thirst for oil, we would make better time in the open sea. Now we were heading for Port Hardy, on Vancouver Island, where we would clear into Canada, then thread our way, through the intricate network of channels between Vancouver Island and the mainland, to the city of Vancouver, where Expo '86 was drawing capacity crowds.

The journey was straightforward, until we closed the land once more. Then rolling fog banks shut out the sun as we groped in toward Queen Charlotte Sound. A radio bearing showed us to be near the southern tip of Moresby Island, which forms the northern edge of the sound. We could hear the sound of breakers on the shore ahead. Suddenly Hilary shouted "I can see the beach, dead ahead." I turned parallel with the shore, I hoped, and went to check the chart. "Watch out carefully ahead," I shouted, "the rocks may extend out toward us." Sure enough, Hilary soon called down "Rocks ahead". I went up to the cockpit again and we steered out carefully to give the rocks a safe clearance. Confident that we were clear of the shoreline now, I went to study the chart once more. Vicki was just getting up to come on watch, the watch change having been delayed as it would make no sense to change over control in the middle of an emergency.

Hilary was watching the vague shape of the coastline to port and scanning the murk ahead. Suddenly Catherine, who was looking through a porthole in the saloon, said calmly "Daddy, there's an island going by to starboard."

I dived back into the cockpit, but really there wasn't much to do. The rocky islet was dimly visible on one side, the rocky shore on the other. They were about half a mile apart and, provided there was nothing in between, we were safely in the middle. Vicki, making uncomplimentary remarks about my navigation, busied herself with the chart and soon established our true position. We were a little way north of our expected track; certainly I had not expected too much from the radio bearing, we had long ago discovered that they could be used only as a rough guide.

In Northern Europe, where marine radio beacons are plentiful and ranges are short, it is possible to get a reasonable cross bearing on two or more beacons, even though the motion of a small craft makes accurate bearings difficult to obtain. In many parts of the world though, there are few beacons, widely scattered, and often the short range, low powered marine beacons are swamped by much more powerful air navigation beacons. Those, even when shown on the charts or lists of radio signals, are often too far away to give an accurate bearing. Frequently they are impossible even to identify.

Later in the morning the mist rolled away and we could see Queen Charlotte Sound stretching away, open before us. We were relieved because, in addition to our unintentional passage inside the small island, two ships had loomed out of the fog, passing by us at a fair speed. They had been well clear of us, but whether that was luck or judgement we could not tell. We had a sophisticated radar reflector, but how well our echo showed up on the ships' displays we couldn't tell. It was unlikely that they would pick us up at more than three miles range; little enough, if the ship was travelling at 20 knots and the radar was not continuously manned. By the time we saw them there was certainly no time to manoeuvre.

In clear sunlight, with a good strong breeze, we sped across the sound. The fog, though, still lurked ominously, far out at sea. It was clear that we would not reach the entrance to the Goletas Channel, behind Vancouver Island, until long after dark. As we approached the channel we would have the Scott Islands to seaward of us; if we strayed too far to the east we might enter the mouth of Queen Charlotte Strait which, though apparently much wider than the Goletas Channel, is rock strewn and difficult to navigate without local knowledge. Our plan was to stand on toward Vancouver Island until our distance travelled put us close to the land; if we could then see the lights on Cape Scott and Hope Island, our position could be accurately plotted and we would continue on course. Otherwise we would turn about, reduce sail and try to sail slowly on the reverse course until dawn.

At dusk the fog rolled in once more, blotting out stars and lighthouses alike. We turned about and reduced sail; our only concern now being to avoid being drifted sideways by the tide, out toward the Scott Islands. Then thunder began, lightning flashed and gusts of wind swirled from unexpected directions. Now we had three radio beacons in range, so we had reasonably hoped to get at least an approximate check on our position from them; but all the set would produce was a crackling hiss, as the air became charged with static electricity. At both mastheads balls of glowing fire shimmered. I called the children to see this phenomenon; it was only much later on that we discovered that Diana could not understand why we were making such a fuss, about what she took to be the masthead lights. Meanwhile Hilary, looking out through the forehatch, discovered that the forestay was covered, down its entire length, with glowing orbs the size of footballs. I had read of the occurrence of "St Elmo's Fire" in the rigging of the great sailing ships, but had never seen it until this spectacular display.

A worrying, if entertaining, night gave way to a grey, fog-shrouded dawn. Lights briefly glimpsed through the murk gave us an approximate position; though both they and the radio beacons which we now began to receive were now at too wide an angle to each other to give an accurate fix. We sailed, motored rather, as the wind had now died altogether, between vertical walls of coiling mist soaring a thousand feet into the air. A rocky peak showed briefly above the fog; to be swallowed at once as the sun rose in a blood red disc above the horizon, increasing the mist immediately to impenetrable thickness and raising it another 500ft. Very slowly and cautiously we edged toward the shore; to our relief another lane through the mist appeared and we were able to motor safely in sight of the land. But what land? After a long time spent scanning that grey and featureless shore, where one hill overlapped the next and the swirling vapour blurred all outlines, distorting perspective, we turned and plodded slowly eastward. Once more we had to consider tidal streams running at up to twice our maximum speed; if we failed to enter the narrows soon we would have to head out for another night in the offing.

Around one more headland, not really seen against the overlapping further shore until we were almost there, the opening appeared at last. Now that we knew exactly where we were, of course, a marker buoy came into view, then a lighthouse and fishing boats. Most important, a breeze came, to push us rapidly over the overfalls as the tide began to turn against us. On our port side, about a mile ahead, lay the entrance to Bull Harbor; a small sheltered inlet, spreading out from a narrow channel to a wide pool surrounded by trees. We reached the entrance before the stream outside gathered strength against us and anchored in late afternoon sunshine, as the mist rolled in to the channel which we had just left, closing the entrance with a blank, white wall.

It was the last bad weather we were to see for months. After clearing into Canada at Port Hardy, where a great black bear strolled casually along the water's edge one day, between the moorings and the houses along the shore, we intended to thread our way through the intricate network of channels between Vancouver Island and the mainland.

Needing to replenish our stores, we made the alarming discovery that there was no bank in Port Hardy which would advance cash on our Master Card. That problem was overcome by Derek, the customs officer, who provided us with transport to Campbell River, 200 miles away. Collecting our cash at the Bank of British Columbia, we discovered that they had, in fact, a branch office in Port Hardy, but it was so obscurely sited that no one there had thought of suggesting it. Still, we had a nice drive and Derek enjoyed the joke when we explained what had happened.

That problem solved and the stores obtained, we could safely venture into the largely unpopulated regions beyond. There were a few worrying stretches, where lack of wind and our low speed under power made it difficult to pass through the rapids and overfalls between one safe anchorage and the next. Only one was really alarming though.

That night, after endless blue days sailing easily in broad channels with a dozen or more orcas, or killer whales, in company, we were threading a narrow cleft between dizzying slopes, unable to pass the next hazard before nightfall. The spot where we had planned to anchor looked less attractive in reality than on the chart, the holding was poor, the rocks loomed close and the depths were too great for our liking. Our next option was not much better, a narrow ledge on the edge of a steep drop, with a hard rock bottom on which our anchor slithered helplessly, seeking a grip. By then, further advance was impossible, as an attempt to stem the tidal stream at full power showed; we were driven backwards at several knots and had to make hastily for a backwater out of the main stream, before we were swept away completely. Finally anchored, we were suddenly swept aground by a vicious eddy which was completely unexpected. We had the dinghy over, taking a line to the shore at the time, so were able to quickly run out a second anchor with that and pull ourselves off. Just as abruptly, we were pulling hard in the opposite direction, away from the shore altogether.

With two anchors out, and a line to a tree ashore, we spent an anxious and wakeful night. The swirling currents heeled us far over; we slackened and tightened lines frequently to ease the strain. By the time the stream turned and the waters became placid again, it was time to get underway in order to reach our next stopping place safely.

Shoal Bay, where we tied to the state float that evening, was a complete contrast. Peaceful and secure, it offered us a chance to catch up on our sleep. There we met Dai and Mary, with their son Sailor, aboard "Ty Bach", whose Welsh dragon flag the children spotted instantly. There also we met George and Darla, in whose lovely home in Santa Barbara we were later to stay. Dan, too, whose photographs of "Dorothy Ann" under sail are among the very few remaining. There was an old, abandoned gold mine in the hills above the bay; we climbed up to peer into its dank and cramped tunnels. Hidden among the trees were the massive stumps of the cedars, hacked off at chest height by the old loggers who tore through this country in an orgy of greed and destruction; even as their modern counterparts, aided by the hideous power of the chain saw, are striving to do to what little remains.

We moved on, in easy waters now, with plentiful safe anchorages and moorings. One night, in a crowded spot, we were hailed by Petra and Graham, from Victoria, who invited us to tie alongside "Saiorse", Petra's beautiful yacht which she built herself, over 10 painstaking years.

The next day we had an opportunity to give help, rather than accepting it, for once. Pat and John, on holiday from Seattle with their family, had run short of fuel; we towed their boat for a little while, whilst John went ashore with the outboard dinghy to get more. It wasn't much of a favour, but we were glad of any chance to give, after so much receiving.

A few more quiet nights and sunny days and we were approaching Vancouver. Carol and Frank had given us tickets to Expo '86; Dai and Mary had invited us to moor as their guests at their marina in False Creek, on the banks of which the Expo site was located.

In the wider waters of the strait of Georgia the wind blew more freely. Sooner than we expected, we were standing in toward English Bay and joining the stream of sightseeing traffic into False Creek. After passing under the two bridges which span the creek we headed a little to starboard of the traffic, to where Dai and Mary, with their friend Bill, were waiting to take our lines and make us fast alongside Bill's boat.

With Mary and Sailor as our guides, we set out to see Expo '86. We had a preview on arrival, as the spectacular firework display which concluded each evening was right in front of the marina. On the site itself we found the pavilions exciting and exhausting.

We discovered that there was a transit mooring within the Expo site, where "Tioga", a beautiful wooden yacht from Everett, in Washington state, was moored. "Tioga"'s crew suggested that we tell the marine section of the Expo staff of our existence. The result was that next morning, as Dai and I were collecting spares from the Yanmar agency, Vicki phoned the shop, telling me to return at once, as we had been invited to move "Dorothy Ann" into Expo.

Because we still needed to keep moving fairly rapidly, we were unable to accept an invitation to spend a period there at a slightly later date, and the berth was only free for two days during our planned time in Vancouver. It was as well. For our two days we were besieged by visitors, talking ourselves happily hoarse, answering their questions. There were many marine exhibits, but most had been transported overland to Expo, and few were manned by people who had sailed them. The notable exception was the replica of Drake's "Golden Hind" which lay alongside us. We took some pleasure in noting that she was built by Hinks, of Appledore, North Devon; just 37 years after "Dorothy Ann" left that same yard.

Tony, the Honorary Local Representative of the Cruising Association, had held our mail for us. Now he came aboard with it, sure of a warm welcome! He bought us a fish and chip supper and complimented us on our tea; no small praise from a Yorkshireman. The following weekend, he and his wife Mary collected us for a visit to the small local airfield, from which they fly their 30 year old Harvard aircraft "Bessy". To our delight and surprise, for we had not expected it, we were all offered a flight. Vicki and I had not flown for almost 20 years; the two smaller children not at all. Catherine's introduction to flying had been from Hawaii to Honolulu and thence, on a jumbo jet, across 1,200 miles of empty Pacific ocean to the tiny dot of Christmas Island. We all enjoyed our day, in the sunlit skies of the Canadian/U.S. border. I was particularly grateful to Mary for giving up her cockpit to me that day, as I had wanted to fly the Harvard from my teenage years, but never had the opportunity earlier.

That evening Ernie and Margaret, who had met us at Expo, had invited us to dinner. So we were driven into Vancouver by Tony and Mary, transferred into Margaret's car, and carried off to her home. It's a good job they all have large cars, as there were not only the five of us, but Mary had pressed a huge box of fruit and vegetables onto us as a leaving present.

From Vancouver south through the San Juan islands, with a brief call on John and Kottie, now living ashore on Pender Island, we wound our way back into the U.S.A. at Friday Harbor. From there it was only a short run to Port Townsend, where we were soon invited to take part in the 10th Annual Wooden Boat Festival. Geoff, keeping the date made in Juneau, came swinging aboard on the final day of the festival, just in time to enjoy the sail-past with the fleet. We sailed on to Edmonds, a small marina just north of Seattle, from where we could visit Pat, John and their family. Vicki took the opportunity to use Pat's kitchen and giant pressure cooker, bottling 74 pint jars of meat. Catherine spent a day at each of two schools, with each of Pat's daughters in turn, furthering her experience of the American educational system. Then to Everett, where we borrowed "Tioga"'s slip for a night, for a last visit to Geoff and other friends whom we had met at Port Townsend.

Next we passed through quaint La Conner, with its restaurants built out over the waterfront and guest docks for customers, to Anacortes, where Kate's other old shipmate, Sue, had invited us to stay. We spent a week with Sue and her husband Joe. They took us high over the Cascade mountains, visiting Joe's parents and calling en route on Michael, a baker and cafe proprietor, in Leavenworth, whom we had met at our barbecue in Spenser Park, Hawaii.

Our time was quickly up and though we would gladly have accepted Sue and Joe's offers of further hospitality we could not afford to spend an extra year on the wrong side of the Panama Canal. Our old friend Jim's family, in Seattle, would also have delayed us in Washington state for the winter, as indeed would Pat and John. Once again we were facing the double dilemma of the traveller. Made welcome by loving and attentive friends, delighting in their wit and flattered by their intelligence, the traveller is only there because he or she travels. To stop is to become a fraud. The second problem is that when it is necessary to keep to some sort of schedule, in our case a simple question of how long we could support ourselves and maintain the boat, time spent with one group of friends must inevitably be taken from others. So many people gave us so much time, and so much love, that we had a constant struggle to try and return even the tiniest fraction of what we received.

And so we went on, to the city named, like so many pubs and railway stations, after our navigator; or so we let her believe.

Victoria, British Columbia, with its ivy covered Empress Hotel and cafes serving cream teas, is a British provincial town, suspended in time. Except that it is peopled with bright, vital Canadians, who are capable of preserving the best of their heritage without being stifled by it. Providing another obvious difference are the float planes, busily taking off and landing on the harbour. A bit disconcerting to sail through until one becomes accustomed to the casual, absolute expertise of the bush pilots.

Moored in the centre of town, we soon heard the familiar "Have you met the people who followed behind you all the way up from Hawaii to Alaska?" query again. "Oh yes, Charlie and Mandy" we casually replied. "No, Charlie and Maggie" came the response. Confusion reigned until it transpired that, yes, this was indeed another couple, with almost identical names, who had also followed in our wake.

Then we were introduced to the Canadian Forces Sailing Association, whose members proceeded to overwhelm us with help and kindness. Thanks particularly to Bill and Alice, Bob and Bev (who had lost their boat on the Oregon coast and, out of all their possessions, managed to salvage only half a brassiere), Dave, Tony and Chris.

As always, there were others no less worthy of mention, but with all our records gone we hope they will forgive us our lapses of memory. With this willing help "Dorothy Ann" was lifted out, scrubbed off and painted once more. Our badly chafed mainsail was repaired and much minor maintenance carried out. Petra, too was there, once we had managed to gain access to the locked and barricaded private marina where "Saiorse" lay. She also offered transport, but we had few stores to collect as we were planning a major restocking in San Diego.

Bob, a one man work force, was everywhere at once. Arranging the haul out, painting the bottom, driving us around town, up the masts, scrounging stores, splicing ropes; it was exhausting just to watch him. When we became exhausted, he and Bev would restore our strength by taking us out to eat.

Once again we were pressed to stay, but had to move on. The berth which we vacated was occupied by Charlie and Maggie's "Kiegenoo". Charlie was recovering from recent surgery and we hoped that our friends at the C.F.S.A. would be able to persuade them not to continue their trip until the next year. We were delighted to learn that they had done so, when Charlie and Maggie, who had flown back to England to work for a spell before resuming their voyage, made the long drive down from Leicestershire to London, to visit us on our return.

Our departure, via the Strait of Juan de Fuca, was uneventful. In the early light, before anyone else was up and about, we slipped quietly away from our moorings and out across the deserted bay. There was some fog, but we were able to keep on a safe course by using the long lines of sport fishing boats as marker buoys; passing from one to the next as they lay at anchor a safe distance from the shore, which appeared dimly, then faded again, as the mists writhed and swirled.

By midday it had cleared, though there was little wind. We were quite content; our main concern having been the possibility of strong headwinds which, funnelled down the strait, would have barred our progress altogether. At Port Townsend, whilst the rest of the crew socialised and enjoyed the show, I had spent most of the time fitting new piston rings, bought in Vancouver, to the Yanmar diesel. To my amazement this had proved totally successful; it had stopped the oil burning completely and restored full power, so now we had no problem in motoring the 70 miles out to the open sea.

14
The Golden Coast

Once clear of the Strait of Juan de Fuca we had wind aplenty. It was a fair wind, too, so we were quite happy even if the ride was a little bumpy. We were making good progress, though it would have been exhausting and frustrating had we been heading north. Not anxious to emulate Bob and Bev's misfortune, on that inhospitable coast, we stood well out to sea. Ashore the weather was very different, as we learned when the radio reported that Eureka, 100 miles to the east of us, had been fogbound for three days, with all air traffic halted.

Nearing Cape Mendocino, which juts out abruptly from the North California coast, we were anxious to sight land and check our position. Accurate sights were difficult to obtain in the rough conditions and the coastline trends to the eastward once past the cape. We wanted to be certain we had passed it before changing course. As we edged cautiously in toward the land, with memories of our close encounter north of Vancouver Island still fresh in all our minds, wisps of vapour swirled toward us, from the familiar grey wall which formed the shoreward horizon. Soon the sun was dimmed and we were straining our eyes anxiously for the first sight of land. Suddenly, there was the cape, towering hugely over us. My heart rate must have doubled in that moment, though in fact we were still 20 miles or more offshore. The cape forms the end of a mountain range rising to 4,000ft and, framed in fog with no means of reference, produced the same impression as, say, Beachy Head seen unexpectedly from three feet away.

About 60 miles short of our destination, the good wind failed us at last. We motored on across an oily swell, in hot sunshine. By the next morning Point Reyes was abeam; we watched in awe as the local fishing boats worked frighteningly close in to the surf, which pounded and smashed against the sheer rock face. Strings of pelicans flew by in line astern, wing beats synchronised with precision, to suddenly plunge into the ocean, resembling nothing so much as a broken umbrella. Amazingly, the umbrellas reassembled themselves on the surface and, with a lumbering run, became smooth flying predators once more.

Just after mid day we were threading the shoals and overfalls which lie to the north of the entrance to San Francisco Bay, To our delight a good west wind sprang up, so we were able to stop the motor and fly our beautiful spinnaker, which Vicki had made in New Zealand. With Catherine at the helm, we swept under the Golden Gate Bridge in fine style; turning to port after passing under the bridge and dropping sail as we ran down easily to anchor, off Sausalito. We lay quietly to the outgoing tide, as evening faded into night and the lights of downtown San Francisco and the Bay Bridge twinkled across the water as from a distant fairyland.

As sometimes happened, we were slow to contact any of the many people whom we knew in the area. Some were away, some had moved house, some just weren't in when we phoned. It made little difference; Mike, Tracy, Jim and Peggy, at Pelican Harbour in Sausalito, quickly came to visit us and make friends. Once more we were being fed and driven around by people whom we had barely met. Of course the children were great ambassadors, especially as, like most children, they could produce better manners for strangers than we ever saw at home. Busy with the unceasing maintenance, I was more or less obliged to leave all but a few social contacts to the rest of the family, so the burden of writing our thanks fell heavily upon Vicki.

Then we located Dave, whom we had first met in Raiatea, in the South Pacific. He was promptly pressed into service, providing transport for a desperately needed run to the laundromat. He had little spare time, so we greatly appreciated his help. Next was Steve, whom we had met in Torrent Bay, New Zealand. Steve took us wine tasting in the Sonoma and Napa valleys. We visited his parents, Art and Marie; discovering that Marie had made a cake, with four candles on it, to celebrate the fourth anniversary of our departure from England.

A van hired from "Rent a Wreck" enabled us to visit the breathtaking Yosemite National Park, where we kept our date with Kris, from Glacier Bay. The most dangerous period of the whole voyage was driving back along the freeway into Oakland, on a Saturday night.

Along the San Francisco waterfront we spotted the catamaran "Gone Troppo", which had been moored astern of us in Auckland, New Zealand. Yelling down an enquiry, over the noise from a nearby helicopter landing area, we were invited aboard by the new owners, Ralph and Nan. That led in turn to another invitation, to eat, drink and talk, talk, talk, at their home in Haight-Ashbury, a district now bearing no signs of its past notoriety as the cradle of the Hippie culture.

For those who may one day wish to entertain a cruising sailor, I can recommend the following style of invitation:

Mrs Benefactor requests the pleasure of the company of:

The Grubby family.

For baths, laundry, drinks and dinner.

Dress: desirable, but not insisted upon.

Time: 6.30 p.m. for about ten-thirty, if we're lucky.

Those unable to rise at the end of the evening may sleep on the floor.

In one form or another that was the gist of the invitations which we constantly received. We could only hope that our "Travellers' Tales" would be thought an adequate recompense for the time, trouble and money which people constantly expended on our entertainment and needs.

We visited the now disused "Alcatraz", the prison for prisoners who would not accept the discipline of other prisons. Shut in the darkness of the punishment cells, reputedly a frightening experience for many, Kate and I both commented on what a pleasant, peaceful sensation it was. Compared with a week of bad weather aboard "Dorothy Ann" a spell in "solitary" didn't seem a very rigorous prospect.

Shrieks of delight from the children informed us that Fred had arrived from Honolulu. He was crewing a large yacht to the Caribbean, and we hoped to catch up with him again in Belize, after our transit of the Panama Canal. Meanwhile, we wore out our jaws with talking over old times. In the next harbour we found another friend from our days in French Polynesia. Mike combines sailing with writing Jewish cookbooks. Now he was seeking a more lucrative means of support, trading in futures by means of an on board computer and a satellite link. It seems that not all of us go to sea to escape the benefits of technology.

We rode the famous cable cars, explored Chinatown, drove with Steve down sinuous Lombard Street and up to the Coit Tower, where a man wearing a rabbit's head was dancing in the fountain; Diana gave him a carrot, which he accepted graciously and ate. "Just another of our normal San Franciscans," said Steve.

Art and Marie came to visit "Dorothy Ann"; then, with the usual abruptness, it was time to go.

During much of our stay the Golden Gate had been wreathed in rolling, coiling fog, though the bay itself usually enjoyed brilliant sunshine. Noting that the fog frequently rolled in at about midday, we timed our leaving as early as the tide permitted. It was none too soon; the fog horns on the bridge were booming above us as we left and out at sea a grey pall hung suspended. Under power and sail we worked out clear of the narrow entrance, turning south into clear weather well before nightfall. As we sailed slowly south, the glittering lights of the bay cities, high on the hillsides, passed slowly in review; San Francisco, Daly City, San Mateo, Redwood City; with the beaches of Pacifica, Moss Beach, El Granada and Half Moon Bay below. The sun-soaked golden coast of California stretched ahead of us for 1,500 miles; we intended to enjoy it.

A brief diversion into Monterey Bay, where we were

made welcome by the Elkhorn Yacht Club, at Moss Landing, enabled us to visit more friends from our stay in Huahine; Howard, Dana and their daughters Cheryl, Jenelle and Danika. Having deprived the children of their party on that earlier occasion in Huahine, I was determined to get them to Moss Landing in time to enjoy Hallowe'en with their friends. We arrived just in time. Their introduction to "Trick or Treat" resulted in a massive haul of chocolate bars and other goodies.

Hallowe'en is a very big event for Americans, deserving the sort of care and preparation which we English devote only to Christmas. Cheryl was dressed becomingly for the occasion, as a replica of one of Dracula's ladies; the outstanding feature being a pair of magnificent fangs, built on so securely by dentist Howard that he had to grind them off the next day.

Once again our stay was all too brief. With a one day visit to Monterey, to feed the sealions from the pier and visit Steinbeck's Cannery Row, we set out for Long Beach Harbor, Los Angeles.

As we headed south, in rising wind and sea conditions, we could hear a rescue operation being carried out about 100 miles to the south of us. Normally we would have been completely unaware of it, as we had insufficient electrical power to keep the V.H.F. radio on all the time and usually switched it on only for the coastguard weather forecasts, or if we wished to transmit to a ship or shore station. On this night though, we had been speaking to a survey vessel which was towing a huge float over a mile astern of it. The skipper had used his searchlight to attract our notice, as the light on the float had failed and we were coming up astern of him, unaware of its presence. It was just as we went to switch off the radio after speaking to him that we heard the coastguard transmitting to the yacht in distress. Because V.H.F. transmissions travel in a straight line, communication between vessels is normally possible over only about 25 miles at best, being cut off after that distance by the curvature of the earth. The coast guard aerials are sited on the mountain tops, giving a much greater range.

Because the coastguard carefully and methodically checked and repeated all the information they were given, we were able to learn that the yacht was somewhere south of the Channel Islands, off Santa Barbara, taking in water and immobilised by a faulty transmission. They may have had some other damage, since there was no shortage of wind where we were, yet they seemed not to be sailing; although possibly on that coast there could have been very different conditions a short distance away. At dawn we would still be 50 miles away from them, more than we would travel before nightfall, even if we continued to head south. It was worrying, knowing of their plight yet being so helpless to assist them. We monitored the V.H.F. anxiously for the rest of the night. Then, to our great relief, the coastguard were able to spot them from an aircraft and direct assistance to them. We would have been unlikely to reach them in time to be of any use, but could hardly have turned east until we knew they were safe. Now we could head in to the Santa Barbara Channel with our consciences clear.

Once inside the channel, sheltered by Point Conception, the wind dropped to a comfortable level as we made our way past the long chain of oil rigs which border the channel. It is necessary to keep within fairly narrow limits, as the areas near and inshore of the rigs contain submerged pipelines, unlit buoys and other hazards. We were navigating just clear of the outbound shipping lane, this being one of the areas in which there are legally enforced separation zones. The inbound lane is the southern one, too close to the Channel Islands for our liking, so we preferred the narrow, inshore zone. It can be a little disconcerting on bends in the channel though, where big ships appear to be coming straight toward one, until they make their turn.

The small harbour at Santa Barbara can be difficult to enter, due to widespread growths of kelp. It is also subject to heavy storms at times. Reading the pilot, we were persuaded that it was not a good stop for us and decided to carry on to Long Beach. By the next evening,

Los Angeles lay before us and we traversed the great sweep of its bay, from Santa Monica to Redondo Beach, past Palos Verdes and San Pedro, to round Point Fermin into San Pedro Bay, at nightfall. It was a calm clear night as we traversed the vast length of Los Angeles harbour, slipped through the entrance, close astern of a container ship and crept cautiously past the enormous mooring buoys used by the cruise liners, to find the entrance to Long Beach Marina.

At 17.50 dollars a night it was the most expensive marina we had stayed in, but we weren't staying long. Ash, an old friend from many years back, drove down with his wife, Barbara, to take us for a tour of Beverly Hills and the parts of L.A. made famous by Hollywood; ending the day with a splendid barbecue at their home. It was a long day, with a lot of driving. I fell asleep on the journey back down the freeway to the marina and thought how Ash, who had done all the driving, still had the long trip home to do. It was typical of the enormous trouble people took, just to provide for our pleasure.

We phoned Darla to say we had passed by Santa Barbara and so we wouldn't be able to visit. "No problem," she said, "I will just drive over and collect you; then you won't be able to leave before I want you to." So we stayed and lazed, letting Darla spoil us completely, in the cool, comfortable home which she and George have created high on the hillside, overlooking the Channel Islands, set in a shimmering blue sea.

An easy sail to San Diego, apart from a brief struggle when we strayed into the great kelp beds at the harbour entrance, brought us to our last U.S. port. We had for once sent a message ahead, to Joe and Cathy, so that we would have a berth waiting for us at the Silver Gate yacht club, where "Viajero" was moored. It was disconcerting to find on arrival that the message had not been passed on, the visitors' moorings being crowded with craft taking part in the weekend's racing, with no space to spare.

We finally found space at the police dock, but for a maximum stay of 10 nights only. There is free anchorage available in the bay and we could have stayed there at no cost; the problem being that we intended to spend much time ashore. It didn't seem too good an idea to leave "Dorothy Ann" swinging at anchor in a tidal channel, used by a mass of shipping, including large U.S. warships, with no one aboard. It was surprising to note that, although the coastguard are most insistent that anchored boats exhibit the correct, though seldom used, day marks for a ship at anchor, they seem to make little attempt to check that anchor lights are used at night. At least, we were surprised at the number of vessels which we saw anchored at night, often close to the main channel, without lights.

The need to set the riding light each night was another reason not to leave the boat unattended at anchor. Some boats, with large storage batteries, used automatic switches to put on their electric lights at night. We could not think of a way to make our kerosene lamp fill and light itself in our absence.

In a mad scramble we rented an enormous 27ft motor caravan, which we soon learned to call an R.V. (short for recreational vehicle) and headed for the Grand Canyon, intending to return, find a new mooring, move "Dorothy Ann" and get to Escondidio, 25 miles or so north of San Diego, in time to spend Thanksgiving with Niels and Becky.

With 1,500 miles of desert road and freeway, across the states of California, Nevada, Utah and Arizona, behind us, we returned triumphantly a week later. Niels' old pickup truck, which he then lent us, seemed like a Mini by comparison with the R.V. Fortunately by now we had become quite used to switching from automatic to manual gearchanging, and driving on the "wrong" side of the road, whilst changing gear with the "wrong" hand, held no terrors, even in San Diego.

We had managed to see Las Vegas, the Hoover Dam, Palm Springs, and the old London Bridge (now at Lake Havasu City) as well as our main objective, the quite indescribable Grand Canyon. From the astonishing sight of the gamblers, oblivious to the breathtaking feats of the high trapeze artists, at Circus-Circus; to the majesty of the great dam; to an evening spent in a swimming pool under the desert stars, to buying turquoise jewelry at an Indian store in the Painted Desert, to the vastness of the canyon, this was America at its amazing, unbelievable best. And so, in its very different way, was the time we then spent with Niels and Becky. A long promised visit to Disneyland, with their daughter Heather, was a great success. With caravan body now attached, the pickup truck became private sleeping quarters for Vicki and myself, whilst the children slept in the house. During the day it became transport for the vast bulk of five months' stores. At the weekend, crammed with children, picnic food and windsurfers, with the four adults in the front, it thundered down the freeway to the lagoons of Ocean Beach.

In our comings and goings Cathy and Joe kept in touch, taking us out to dinner in downtown San Diego, where the waterfront is crowded with an exotic mixture of working and historic craft. Darwin too, our old shipmate in the Mediterranean, had found us. He swept us off in his usual overwhelming manner, to meals and outings, striding through Balboa Park or along the beach, with the children crowding around him; taking us to visit his brother, Doug, who, with his wife Mary and daughter Amber, treated us like members of the family.

Joe and Cathy managed to arrange a mooring at the Silver Gate eventually, which meant we could load stores without endless ferrying in the dinghy, and get hot showers afterward. The children were more often aboard "Viajero" than "Dorothy Ann", watching T.V. (Joe had even lent them his portable set on the trip to the Grand Canyon) and looking after "Bosun" the budgerigar.

With so many old friends to see, we had little time to meet new ones. Tim and Karen, with their son Joel, deserved more of our time in return for their friendship and help. Tim doesn't just offer; whilst one is dithering over whether it would be polite to accept help, he just does it anyway. Joel and our children were able to spend endless hours together, agreeing on the iniquities of parents and the prehistoric oldness and uselessness of everything and everyone but themselves, which made them all feel much better.

Time raced relentlessly by until we found ourselves, almost as if propelled by some outside power, slipping away from the Silver Gate on an utterly still, moonlit evening, bound for Mexico.

Sand, sun-hats and sight-seeing aboard their "ships of the desert" – impressive, but actually led by 10-year-old Arab boys

Crabs are Diana's only competitors for space on the shores of Christmas Island in the Pacific

15
Heading for Home

People often asked us "When will you be going home?" The answer really was that we had been going home since we left New Zealand, but we were making a few calls on the way. San Diego however, was our last major west coast port, at which we could replenish the bulk of our stores at reasonable prices. In a way then, we were going home from San Diego. True, we still had some calls to make on the east coast, no less important than those on the west. But once through Panama we had only one major crossing to complete and, though the Atlantic was not to be taken lightly, it should not be a very lengthy trip.

We intended, if we could keep to our schedule, to work our way up to Halifax, Nova Scotia and cross from there to Shannon, in southern Ireland. The winds on that northerly route should be strong, but mostly in our favour; just the sort of weather which "Dorothy Ann" performed best in. Our only problem was to ensure that we had all we needed on board for the period between leaving the west coast of the U.S.A. and arriving on the east coast. So we had taken advantage of the chance to stock up in San Diego, where the availability of Neil and Becky's truck meant that we could visit cut price warehouses and buy in bulk. Not a practical proposition if you have to walk several miles to the docks with your purchases. Dennis, in Auckland, had enabled us to do the same thing, so successfully that some of those stores were still aboard.

Water too is heavy, as anyone who has carried a five gallon can of it half a mile, barefoot, down a shell beach can testify. It can be a nuisance too, trying to fill many cans from a slow tap, which others need to use. In

Huahine it had sometimes taken three hours to fill a five gallon can from the only tap on the beach. On other occasions, no water came out at all. Washing out and refilling all tanks and cans from a marina hose may not be very adventurous, but it does leave some energy for real adventure, if the chance arises; we were grateful to be able to do that chore at the Silver Gate.

On a small boat, everything which is carried prevents some other thing from being carried. So if more fuel is to be taken aboard, the space which could have held more water is taken up. In a flat calm we might motor 70 miles on five gallons of fuel, in 24 hours. Five gallons of water would last the five of us for two days normally, four at a pinch. If we had wind at all, other than dead ahead, we might hope to make two knots, say 200 miles in four days. Our normal scheme was to carry 180 gallons of water and 20 gallons of diesel fuel. We had a couple of cans in the cockpit which would hold an extra 10 gallons of diesel if we were expecting calms or a long inshore passage. We also had 10 gallons of kerosene for cooking and lighting, plus a five gallon reserve in the cockpit.

We had caught up on our schedule and were leaving San Diego as early as possible after the end of the hurricane season to the south. This would give us the maximum possible time to transit the Panama Canal and travel north to New Orleans before the start of the West Indies hurricane season. The winds should be satisfactory until we reached the latitude of Guatemala; after that we might expect calms and light variables, so we would carry extra fuel when we left Mexico. Few of the Central American countries are safe to venture near, so we expected to travel at least as far as Costa Rica before getting more fuel, water or supplies. If we were fortunate enough to have good winds, we would make for Panama direct.

The only major hazard in our path was the Gulf of Tehuantepec, where northerly winds, funnelled through between the mountains which stretch across to the Gulf of Mexico, on the opposite coast of the continent, reach immense velocities. I could see no reason to even approach this notorious area. A direct course from just south of Acapulco to Costa Rica would keep us well to seaward of it and, if the effects reached out that far, we would simply be blown further away from the worst area. There was a slight temptation to stay further inshore, as if the winds fell light there was some likelihood of alternating land and sea breezes, as the deserts ashore heated and cooled in their daily cycle. The real foolishness though was that we TOOK ADVICE.

Fishermen, delivery skippers, the local cruising guide which we were lent, everyone whom we asked and many whom we didn't, all gave the same advice. "Stick well inshore, sail with one foot on the beach" they chorused, "the wind will be strong but there won't be room for the sea to build up so you will be sailing in quite smooth water." Why we didn't see the obvious, glaring stupidity of this idea is hard to say. I suppose we believed that they were speaking from experience, rather than idly theorising.

But that was still a long way ahead. First we ran 800 miles easily down the side of the great peninsula of Baja California; celebrating another Christmas at sea on the way. This year, having left our friends so near to the festival, we were almost buried in presents and Mary had provided all sorts of good things to eat. We reached Cabo San Lucas, our entry port to Mexico, at the very tip of the peninsula, after a pleasant and enjoyable voyage. The authorities were relaxed and helpful, the anchorage was safe, if a little open to the swell and the beach was superb. The children found their friends aboard "Havelar", who had been in San Diego with us; George and Cherie somehow coping with the temporary doubling of their ship's complement. We tried our first Margaritas (ugh!) and enjoyed the hot sunshine.

After a week's stay we set off again on the slightly longer run to tiny Puerto Angel (pronounce that An,schhell, if you want a Mexican (or Mehican) to understand it.) In fact if you want to be understood at all, south of Acapulco, you had better be able to speak Spanish. Our six weeks in Vigo, four years earlier, had not given us complete mastery of the language, so it came as no surprise to discover that our attempts to clear in to the port had resulted in our being cleared out instead. It didn't really matter, we only wanted fuel and water and the Mexicans weren't about to throw us out if we didn't leave exactly on time; probably they would have been amazed if we had. We discovered where fuel might be obtained and commanded a taxi to take us there. The fare was probably exorbitant by local standards, but it really wasn't much, so we didn't haggle very firmly. We collected the fuel, topped up our water and set out happily for Panama.

16
Disaster

For once there were no farewells to make, no tides to consider, no last minute problems. We were fit and rested; ready to go. Motoring out of the little bay, we found a strong, favourable wind blowing from the west. With this we could have sped safely on our way, laying a course direct for Costa Rica, but no! We knew better. We had ADVICE to guide us. Hugging tightly to the coast we turned eastward and brought the wind astern. Night fell; the wind dropping gradually but still pushing us steadily along, until about 3 a.m. It died away then and we changed watches with the spars clattering; sails flapping idly, outlined against the starry sky.

It was not long before the wind came again, out of the east this time, softly at first but steadily increasing. We were well into the gulf by then, a little further offshore than we wished to be, so I chose to tack to the northeast, where the outline of the mountains was faintly discernible in the false dawn. I held the course until the sound of breakers was clearly audible ahead. Then, far too late, the essential foolishness of the whole plan became evident. I must tack, therefore I must turn away from the shore. If the wind blew from due north there was no problem, we would have it abeam, our best point of sailing, and be able to pick our course, close in to the shore. But it was blowing from the northeast now and strengthening. The so plausible ADVICE, in which we had trusted, was impossible to follow.

On the next watch change we held a conference. Clearly a "Norther" was blowing, but the wind must fan out after passing through the mountains, so it would probably shift through north to northwest as we crossed the centre of the gulf. "We shan't get anywhere hammering into this closehauled," I said, "it's already blowing force six or more and we will just be pushed sideways into the middle of the gulf. We must either turn south of east and make the best speed we can, which will eventually bring the wind astern and get us into the lee of the far shore, or turn to the west and run back." We didn't suppose anything very terrible was likely to happen, but we knew that we would get an awful beating if we went on. It was just a question of whether we were willing to put up with deck leaks and violent motion for a day or two. If we thought for a moment that the boat might not stand up to the weather, we would never have left port to start with.

My own inclination was to press on. Once one starts to run away from a little bad weather, where does it stop? I avoid it if I can, but when it comes I expect to live with it. Vicki is obviously of the same mind. "Oh, we'll carry on, I think" she said with a shrug and took over the watch, easing the sheets a little and bearing away to head east by south.

When I next came on deck we were travelling fast, with the wind still abeam. The seas had built up quite a bit and were breaking regularly. "Dorothy Ann" was coping with most of them, but being slammed hard now and then. We were carrying more sail than we needed, putting unnecessary strain on the boat. I would have dropped the mainsail soon, in any case, but a small tear starting in the reefed mizen prompted me to do so at once, whilst I still had the mizen set to steady us.

The wind began to gust violently as I struggled to get the mainsail lashed down. Catherine clipped on her line and came to help me, but it was very slow work, with the gusts increasing in force as we worked. By the time it was done the tear in the mizen had lengthened considerably. Someone was going to have a big sewing job to do when this was over. I hauled it down, roping it well to boom and gaff, then lashed the tiller a little to starboard.

With the mizen off as well we couldn't expect to sail with the wind abeam, but anyway I wanted to bring it further aft to reduce the impact of the seas on the hull.

With just our small staysail set forward, we still sailed at five knots, but to the southeast now. Things stayed very much the same then, till after nightfall. People lay about reading, drinking tea, sleeping. Every now and then we would roll well over to starboard, as we hung on the face of a comber, then the breaking crest would fall on our exposed topsides with a crash like solid rock. It was probably the worst breaking sea I have ever seen in deep water; well clear of the shore now, we had half a mile of ocean beneath our keel. Nonetheless, we were riding it easily. The impacts were no worse than many we had received before, though rather more frequent perhaps. We had seen higher seas, though none so steep at this height. In short, no one was worried but we would all be thankful when it was past.

Then came another roll, a little further perhaps than any previous one; but this time we seemed to hang for a long time, two or three seconds maybe, on our side, before rolling upright again. That in itself alarmed no one, but I had been careful to keep the small quantity of water collecting in the bilges pumped out, so that it would not slosh about over the floorboards as we rolled; now, though the pump had just sucked dry, there was water over my feet.

That was alarming. No water had come through the hatchway. The bilges were quite deep and had been empty a moment before. 200 gallons or more of water had rushed in from somewhere below. If it continued at that rate, we would sink in minutes. I began pumping at once, naturally, but the water kept rising and soon washed some debris into the pump filter, as I realised when the action of the pump stiffened. It seemed a waste of time to clear it then, it would probably keep clogging and we could bail faster with a bucket, now that the water was quite deep. It was sensible to have the pump mounted where it could be reached from the cockpit or below, but it meant that anyone using it would block the hatchway, so we couldn't bail and pump as well.

There was an electric pump, but that, like so many expensive toys, had broken early in the voyage. Though it was new, no spares were available and though I eventually managed to patch it up, it found an endless number of reasons to malfunction. It mattered little, since the genius who had designed the engine electrical system had mounted both starter and alternator at the lowest point, ensuring that the batteries were shorted out within minutes.

Catherine pushed by and stationed herself in the cockpit. All I had to do was to fill a bucket from floor level and throw it into the cockpit. Kate bailed it overboard from there. Now and then a wave broke over her, soaking her to the skin and refilling the cockpit.

For a while we held the water level, then, after some more pounding by the sea, it rose once more. Again we held it steady, though the level never fell despite all our efforts. The children were up to their chests in water. I made one effort to check the inside of the hull, in one of the few places where access to it was not obstructed by cabin furniture or ballast. The mass of swirling water and floating objects knocked me off my feet as I stooped and probed in the darkness, submerging and choking me. The chance of finding the leak was poor, the chance of reducing it, if found, even less. There was no time to spend on poor chances. We could not hope to bail at that rate for ever. The sea temperature was low and we were becoming chilled and exhausted. Leaving Vicki to take over the bailing I went forward, not without apprehension, and lowered the remaining sail.

I had hoped that the reduced strain with the sail off might lessen the leak, but there seemed to be no improvement. Leaving Vicki to bail once more, with Diana keeping the bailing area clear of floating debris and Hilary getting the emergency packs for the liferaft ready to go, I went forward on deck again. My last hope of saving "Dorothy Ann" lay in rigging a sea anchor, to swing the bows into wind. Perhaps, if the damage were on the windward side, that might reduce the leak. I tied a bunch of old motor tyres, kept on deck as fenders, on to the main anchor. Then I let anchor and chain out, to drag in the water ahead of us. It didn't work. The windage of the mainmast was enough to keep the bows from coming up into wind. Had there been time to set the mizen trysail it might have worked, but it was a faint chance and there was no time left.

Catherine had gone below, cold and exhausted. When I got back to the cockpit it was full of water, so I snatched up a bucket and began to bail. After only a few strokes I saw, in the fluorescent glow of the breaking waves, that water was flowing back in over the starboard side deck.

Instantly it was necessary to make a sharp mental adjustment, not the easiest task when you are cold, tired and, if you had time to admit it, terrified. Until that instant I had been committed to saving the boat, by any and every means I could think of. Now one good sized wave over the stern would be enough to flood and sink her, with Vicki and the children trapped below. From that moment I must think only of getting them safely away in the liferaft.

Anyone who has read the harrowing accounts of the Fastnet race disaster will know that taking to a liferaft in a bad sea is far from easy; even when safely aboard, there is no guarantee that the craft will survive the frightful power of wind and sea. A good friend of ours once said "Only when the liferaft is floating higher in the water than your boat do you climb into it. You climb UP into a liferaft."

He was, we believe still, absolutely correct. The awful dilemma is how to judge the critical point at which there is no hope of saving the ship. I had left it to the utmost limit of safety and wondered if in fact it was already too late. Later I was amazed to find that four hours had elapsed since the leak had started; we had only seemed to spend a few minutes at each task. I had given few orders, we had discussed emergency procedures often in the past and everyone had a good idea of what was necessary. It was as well. Communication was difficult, there was no time for queries or discussion. Everyone did their best and their best was superb.

Confusion would certainly have been fatal. I forced myself to call loudly but clearly down to Vicki to get everyone on deck, waiting to make sure I was heard and understood, though I was frantic to release the liferaft before it was too late. The white casing of the raft showed up clearly, but the lashings securing it to the deck were invisible in the near darkness. I found them with my fingers, guiding my knife with the fingertips and trying to cut line and not flesh. The line parted and I slid the heavy canister easily down the sloping deck to the starboard rail.

I couldn't lift the canister over the low toe rail; my wet, numbed fingers could not grip the smooth glassfibre surface. Vicki had brought the children out, clipped together by their safety harnesses. She came forward over the hatch to help me, just as water began to slop inward over the main deck. The water lifted the canister effortlessly over the toerail, allowing us to push it quickly clear. We pulled on the painter, pulled and pulled and prayed that the inflation system would work. There was a sudden muffled bang as the canister split apart and vanished into the seething water, then nothing. Our hearts sank.

Meanwhile there were problems for the children, as "Dorothy Ann" began to go down by the stern and waves washed over the cockpit as they stood on its edge. Catherine's safety line became entangled, she was held down and submerged as the water swept across the stern. The raft stores which she held were swept away, as she struggled to get free. Hilary, by some miracle, realised what had happened, plunged under water and untangled the line from around the engine controls. She had saved them all from being dragged under as the boat sank, but to do so she was forced to let go of the remaining emergency stores.

By that time Vicki and I could see the dim outline of the inflated raft alongside. We boosted Diana on top of the raft to find the entrance, as "Dorothy Ann" began to sink below the surface. At the last moment I realised that my safety line was still clipped to the line on "Dorothy Ann"'s port side. Leaning across, my hand already under water, I snapped it free. As "Dorothy Ann" went down our lifejackets supported us and we clung to the ropes attatched to the liferaft's sides. It was eerie to see the masts and rigging slowly sinking down alongside us, jet black against the pale glow of the milky way. The box containing most of our flares drifted past, but I hadn't the energy to reach it and it was soon out of sight.

Even as she sank, "Dorothy Ann" protected us from the real force of the sea. We were able to scramble into the liferaft before we were exposed to the full weight of the storm but then, before we could look around or begin to take in our new surroundings, we were struck with immense force and overturned. That was a bad moment. To be snatched from apparent safety, however fragile, and plunged back into danger, is far worse than facing the danger in the first place. Choking in salt water, tangled in each other's limbs, confused and disoriented, we hardly knew how to help ourselves. Then we got our heads above water once more, our eyes adjusted to the faint glow from the canopy light, now under water beneath us, and we realised we were still inside the raft, which was intact though inverted. The knowledge that everyone was together and unharmed overcame the tendency to despair. We bunched ourselves together on one side, threw our weight backwards and righted the raft. Spreading out quickly into a circle, with me at the windward side, we tried to distribute the weight so that the raft would be more stable. It swung round a few times, but finally settled down with the wind on my back. There was a lot of water inside and our first concern was to bail it out. That was difficult because, as we tried to empty water out of the flap in the canopy, more was often driven in from the outside. Even when the canopy door was closed, water was frequently driven in around the edges, so we could never get the floor completely dry.

We were in about 17 degrees north latitude, well below the Tropic of Cancer, but even in the tropics the winter sea temperature is quite cold. Without the canopy we would soon have suffered badly from exposure; as it was, I began to experience painful cramp in the legs after a short time. We reviewed our situation and planned how best to use what assets we had.

Although we had planned and prepared against such an emergency, certain vital aspects had been overlooked. Without practising in a situation so close to the real thing as to be equally hazardous, it is unlikely that those points would be obvious. We had provided water, emergency transmitter, navigation equipment, solar stills, fishing gear, and a host of other equipment, but no means of clipping the packages simply to the lifelines on boat or raft. So they could not be brought out on deck early without being swept away and had to be held and carried into the raft, rather than clipped quickly to the ropes on the outside. As a result, in the wild conditions, all had been lost, as had our passports, money, credit cards and travellers cheques.

Fortunately we had a survival kit packed inside the raft itself. I say fortunately because, although we had ordered the raft to be supplied with the kit enclosed, we had originally received one without it. It would have been very easy, in the chaos of preparation, to have overlooked that fact and lashed down the canister all unknowing that no equipment was inside. Vicki did read the paperwork though and saw the omission. Even then it was tempting to say "Oh there isn't time to change it now" and hope for the best. We did send it back and we did have it regularly serviced, by authorised dealers. At the time, it felt like throwing away desperately needed money, as did paying our insurance premiums!

Soon we learned another lesson. The loss of our money and passports may have helped to save our lives. Although the raft never overturned again, it was frequently bent double by the force of the waves, so that half of us would be thrown with great violence on top of the others. If we had succeeded in bringing the waterproof steel ammunition box containing our valuables aboard, it might have injured someone and would almost certainly have damaged the raft or its canopy. Even a small tear in the canopy would soon have allowed the wind to destroy it; without the canopy, in that wind,

Stillness and sun replace the usual cold mists of Glacier Bay

"How shall we be rescued?" After 17 hours adrift the family peer hopefully from their liferaft; help is at hand (*Joe & Nicky Partridge/ Associated Press*)

death by hypothermia would not have taken long. Don't take sharp or heavy items into the liferaft!

Another thing which we had not thought out was the provision of clothing for use in the raft. All our warm clothing was packed away. We went barefoot. At the time when the emergency began, I was clad in a pair of swimming trunks and Vicki's waterproof jacket (mine having been mislaid). The children had done their best to collect warm clothing from what could be reached in the ready use lockers; a pair of long trousers which I had fortuitously worn, to prevent sunburn and chafe, whilst working at the masthead in Cabo San Lucas, an old woollen cardigan, used on chilly night watches, and two souvenir tee shirts completed my ensemble. Vicki and the three girls each had trousers and sweater; I returned Vicki's jacket to her. It was barely enough; wet through, we all shivered and Catherine was sick.

We had our lifejackets also, which are warm to wear, but eventually we decided that it was better to sit on them, out of the small puddles which inevitably formed around our bottoms no matter how well we bailed and sponged. We hadn't thought of footwear and probably could not have found any if we had, so all of us still had bare feet. That was fine on "Dorothy Ann"; on the raft they were icy.

Packed inside a small canvas bag, safely tied inside the raft, were a bailer, two sponges, torch and spare batteries, fishing gear, paddles, first aid kit, eight half-litre cans of water and five flares. Hilary had managed to bring some fresh fruit and a can of peaches, "because it contains more liquid" she explained. She had read also that people became very bored in liferafts, so she had brought some books, her descant recorder and her sheet music. In the chaos and semi-darkness of the final moments below decks, she had not been able to be very selective. Our literary choice included Conrad's "Lord Jim", "Tales of Ancient Egypt" and "Butterflies and Moths of the British Isles". No doubt, had we been less fortunate, we would have become glad of all of them.

We had no food, simply because digestion requires

water, and we would die of thirst long before we would suffer any hardship from starvation. Somewhere in the sea around us floated a 10 gallon drum of water, which I had released overboard, but the storm would separate us from that and from the other items which must still have been near us in the darkness and confusion, at first. Vicki had also tried to bring two water cans aboard, but the line by which she was holding them had snagged, as they washed to and fro in the chaos below decks, and she had not dared to return below to free it.

Our chances of being saved depended entirely on the careful use of our five flares. Steamers cross the mouth of the gulf, which we were blowing toward; fishing boats ply inside, as we had noted before the storm. The raft would be all but invisible at less than half a mile, in full daylight on a calm sea. A parachute flare, of which we had only two, would be visible for miles, especially at night, but would not indicate our exact position. We had three hand-held flares which were intended to guide rescuers to us.

One other item of equipment was a drogue, or sea anchor. This is designed to act like a parachute in the water, stopping the raft from being blown rapidly downwind and keeping the entrance pointing away from the weather. We did not use it at first, for two reasons. Firstly, we were anxious not to cause any more resistance to the wind than we could help, to minimise the strains on the raft, secondly, we wanted to blow toward the shipping lanes. We thought that it would be about 15 hours before we would be in the path of the shipping along the coast; we would put the drogue out then, to try and stay among the shipping as long as possible. We would not use our flares until a vessel was within half a mile and facing toward us, unless we sighted one just before dawn, when our flares would be most visible, to attract attention, and the search for our actual position would take place in daylight. There was no point in attempting to look out until conditions moderated; standing up in the entrance would endanger the raft and nothing could be seen except the next wave.

We bailed and talked. Daylight came and we stopped shivering. Survival, we decided, would depend largely on our having the will to keep trying everything at our command. As one or the other of us showed signs of flagging, the others would shout "WILL, you MUST have WILL" which got everyone smiling again. We set a lookout, though the seas were still too high to allow much visibility, except when we balanced briefly on the larger crests. The others dozed fitfully. Hilary knelt, peering through the slightly open door flap. Green pyramids of water rose and fell hypnotically before her. Sometimes she had a view of white flecked, glassy seas, stretching away to a ragged, empty horizon. The sun, already well past the zenith, hung in a brassy blue sky. And there before her, as the raft rose yet again to rock and sway over a crest, was a large, black ship.

"A ship, a ship!" Hardly had she spoken when Vicki shot past her, tugging at the cords securing the flap, to stand, teetering and swaying, in the entrance. I was already trying, with bleached and shrivelled fingers, to open the bag containing the precious flares. It was 15 hours since we had entered the raft.

PART THREE ... AND AFTER

17
Rescue

It was the Korean container ship "Rainier". She was travelling fast, already abeam of us. I handed Vicki a parachute flare, she snatched off the end caps and pulled the igniter cord. Nothing happened!

We were dumbfounded. The flares were wet, but surely flares are intended to withstand wetting? Besides, such devices have been known to light after a delay. Rocking and swaying as we were, it might be pointing anywhere by then, injuring one of us or even destroying the raft. I passed Vicki a hand flare and grabbed the parachute flare, which I tried to keep pointing away from us all. After a little while, I threw it into the water.

We could now see "Rainier"s stern, as she headed rapidly away toward Panama. "What do we do if they don't see this one?" said Vicki, holding the flaming red hand flare aloft. "We wait for a better chance" I said, "with only three flares left, some more of which may not work, we can't risk wasting them on a boat which is going away from us." The flare spluttered out. We had none of our signalling mirrors aboard, but I grabbed a can of water and tried to use the shiny base to catch the sun. I waved my red tee shirt in the other hand, Vicki holding me upright, and screamed, though I knew the sound was too feeble to be heard.

Even "Rainier"s stern was vanishing now and I began to lose hope, until I realised why. She was turning. Round she came in a great swinging circle toward our position. But we still had not deployed the drogue and we were drifting fast downwind. As the ship approached we were carried forward toward her towering bows. Watching helplessly, we saw the great steel wall rushing toward us, the huge anchor hanging menacingly above. Then a wave ahead of us broke against the ship's side and a mass of water curled over and down, flattening us into the bottom of the raft, but driving it clear of the ship. We whirled aft along the ship's side and spun away astern.

We awaited events. It was a long way from sea level to "Rainier"s decks, though, even so, the sea threw spray over them. We wondered how we would get up there and made our own plans, assuming that they would float a line down to us. It seemed unlikely that they could recover a boat safely, if one were launched in an attempt to reach us. Nothing much seemed to be happening now. "Rainier" steamed around at a safe distance and hooted encouragingly. People on the stern waved. I began to suspect that help was being summoned from another source. "I think he's radioing for help" I said to the others and began to search the far horizon.

Though quite harmless now, the waves were still fairly big, so it took some time to glimpse the whole horizon. Not knowing in which direction to look, I was obliged to keep scanning all the way round, so the onrushing white hull was well in view by the time I spotted it and told the others. As it drew closer the excitement became intense. "Could it be 'Island Princess'?" we wondered. Vicki had been aboard that P & O liner in Skagway and our largest Red Ensign was a gift from her. No, this ship had twin funnels. "I believe it's one of ours, anyway," I said. "I think it might be "Canberra". No, of course not, that would be absurd!"

As the ship drew nearer, I was able to see without standing up, so I moved across to watch through the ventilation trunk, opposite the doorway. That allowed the others to crowd over and look out through the flap. "It is 'Canberra' you know" said Vicki.

Handled superbly, "Canberra" was stopped dead upwind of us, where she would protect us from wind and wave and drift gently sideways toward us. The manoeuvre, perfectly executed at the first attempt, looked easy. Putting a 45,000 ton ship alongside a six foot diameter rubber raft, without harming the occupants, is not quite that simple. It is only the skill, developed by

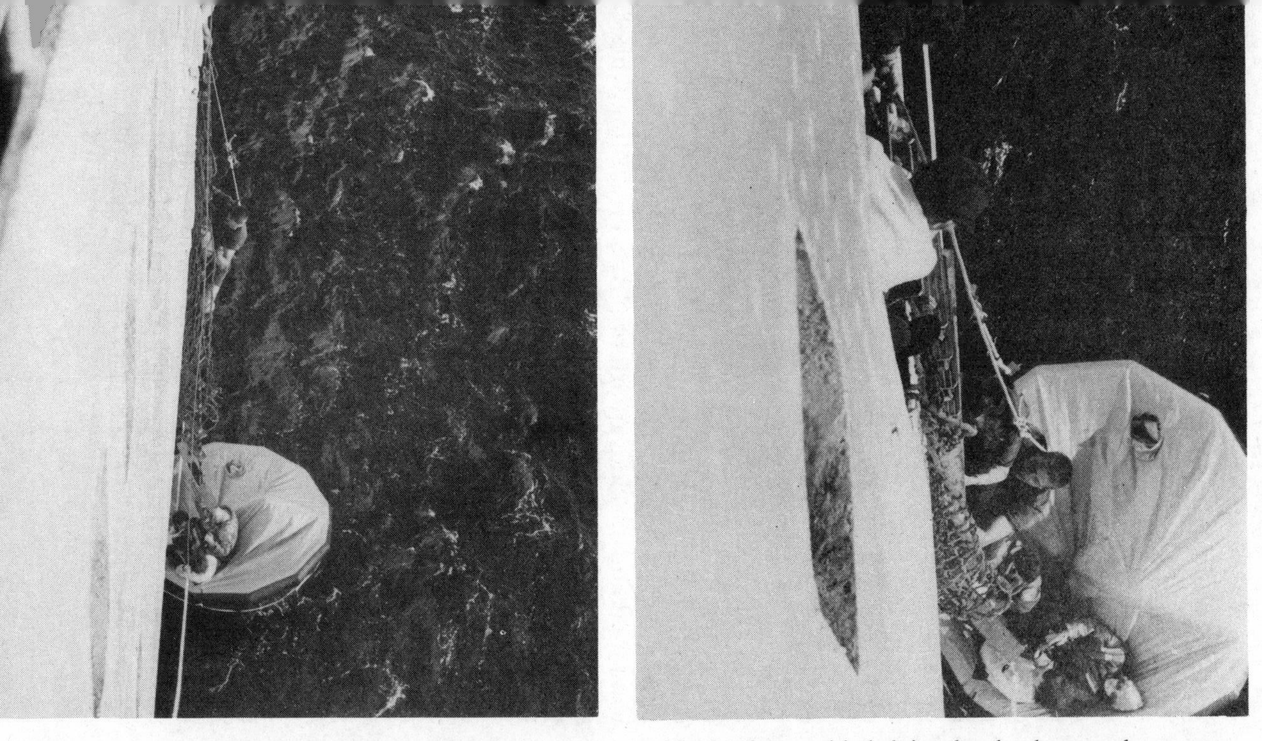

It's a long way to climb; the family prepare to scale "Canberra"'s sheer side (*Joe & Nicky Partridge*)

Nearly there; with helping hands above and seaman Tim's strong arms, the family make their final ascent to safety (*Joe & Nicky Partridge/Associated Press*) years of training and experience, of the captain and his crew, which makes it seem so.

We contributed our mite, deploying the drogue to keep us more or less stationary until we were safely alongside. With ropes to catch, a net, a ladder, safety lines and the helping hands of Tim, the young giant seaman stationed at the foot of the ladder to help us, our safety was assured. As 2,000 passengers and crew lined the rails in silent awe, we were helped aboard, wrapped in blankets and hurried to the ship's hospital. Our raft, too, was brought on board, whilst we were given hot baths and drinks, medical checks and the first of many superb meals. It was, as someone later remarked, an elegant rescue.

On board the raft we had played a game of "How shall we be rescued." "By a Mexican fishing boat" had few supporters, though it seemed most likely and we would certainly have been most grateful for our lives. "By a tanker" was a popular choice. They have reputation for good food and spacious quarters. "By a cruise liner" was considered frivolous and not to be seriously contemplated! Now, thanks to P & O, our adventures had a fairytale ending.

At a time when our egos were very fragile and criticism would have hurt us badly, "Canberra"'s captain and crew gave us their unqualified support. The passengers too, welcomed us and hastened to supply Vicki and the girls from their own wardrobes. Expecting only to be carried to the first port of call and put ashore to fend for ourselves, we were invited to travel with the ship to Los Angeles, from where P & O arranged for our flight home. The passengers contributed a substantial sum to meet our immediate needs, which eased the problems of returning from tropical Mexico to London at seven degrees below freezing point.

Press and T.V. were polite and easy to deal with, in the main. They printed few errors, though those which were made were widely circulated. More importantly, many of our friends, whose addresses we had lost, saw the story and wrote at once. Some went to enormous trouble to trace us and the indefatigable Darwin drove the 120 miles from San Diego to Los Angeles, to claim the right to drive us to the airport. He also paid us, there and then, for the first copy of this book.

The first week in London was chaos. Press and T.V. interviews, meeting relatives and friends, arranging school for the children, shivering, coughing and sneezing in our first English winter for four years, we hardly knew where we were. Then, just as suddenly, we were forgotten; we could begin trying to resume our lives.

18
One More Time

Slowly we are collecting our few scattered belongings, from attics and sheds up and down the country. "Dorothy Ann" was insured, though not for sufficient to replace her, far less what she contained. But we are not destitute. We will get a home, in time, collect the family together again and settle down to the routine of work.

We still don't look any different from anyone else. The children are larger and so are our debts; our car is smaller and singular. But we found the magic door; we know what lies behind it. One or two people have asked us "How can you take such a risk, especially with the children?" Sitting in "Canberra"'s radio office, waiting for the many press calls, I had ample time to catch up on the world's news, by satellite T.V. "Mad axeman murders family in Sydney" I remember, with many items of like nature. Near Los Angeles airport, a huge hoarding exhorted local residents to take action, to "Catch the Strangler". At home, a young lout, driving at over 80mph in a residential street, collided with a parked car, killing the occupant and escaping unscathed. The judge released him because "After all" he said, "he hadn't been drinking!" I would have thought paralytic drunkenness was the only imaginable mitigating factor and I wonder whom to fear most, the lunatics in the street or the imbeciles on the Bench. If we had returned voluntarily we might well ask "How can we subject our children to the risks of life on land?"

No, the physical risks don't worry us because we can see that they are less than we face daily on land. Many people are at far greater risk on the roads every day, as accident figures show. They simply pretend the risk is not there. In industry and even in the home, tragic accidents occur. Is driving thousands of miles on a motorway, to be crushed by a 40 ton truck, better than sailing from New Zealand to Alaska, with a slight risk of drowning?

We may die any day; we certainly will some day. The question is, how to live until then? Education is a problem. Vicki worked hard to keep the children up to standard, but felt that they needed better facilities and equipment for their secondary schooling. We had always intended that they should return to school in time to prepare for their public examinations, so that they would have the maximum number of choices in their future careers. We don't mind what they want to do, we just want them to be able to do it. It came as a shock to find that, back in a regular school, they had insufficient work to do and complained that they were given no homework. With the system in further disarray through teachers' strikes, we are now forced to consider paying privately for their education.

We have also discovered that our absence abroad has disqualified us from receiving unemployment benefit or family allowance, though had we simply sat here and done nothing these would have been ours by right. Luckily for us we had the money given to us aboard "Canberra" to support us for a little while, with friends and family helping out. Our eyes have been opened though and we realise that the security which we thought was the one redeeming feature of the "Welfare State" is a complete sham. Good. The sooner we can get out of it again, the better.

But those are the bad things, the petty irritations created by petty people. It would be a terrible mistake to waste valuable time fretting over them; they are best thrust aside, though we should take any passing opportunity to harm the perpetrators. What matters is that out there, through the magic door, there is a cleaner world, full of beauty, warmth and love. And the door is still ajar, because our friends have rallied round, with letters, photographs, phone calls and visits; keeping our memories alive as we struggle to find our feet and make our way back again.

Many of them, also, are struggling to overcome difficulties, pay off debts, find new partners, repair boats or establish themselves in some new venture. The trying may be more important than the doing. It is fashionable to jeer at the old Public School ideal that the way the game is played is more important than the result, but it makes a lot of sense to us. So many people have said "Oh how I would love to do what you are doing, but of course I have my business/family/responsibilities to consider." Which we would generally translate as "I will never do anything interesting or exciting because I am too busy getting rich quick at someone else's expense and anyway I don't like getting wet, cold, tired, hungry or frightened."

I am struggling here to express something so simple, yet which seems to require the gifts of Lawrence of Arabia to define. When we work for money we can be robbed or cheated and end up with nothing for our pains. When the reward is experiences, sensations, feelings, however brief, they cannot be taken away or devalued. The most priceless treasure of all, friendship and love, exists in a bottomless seam which extends throughout all humanity. We do not need to sail, or even to travel afar, to find it, but we are sailors and the story of our travels is the gift which we humbly bring, to lay at the feet of our friends.

For them, above all, we shall sail again.